SALON
SUCCESS
SECRETS

Book 1
A Half-Million Job Openings

KIM STEVENS

Copyright © 2004 by Kim Stevens

ISBN 978-0-7414-1932-3

Published by:

PUBLISHING.COM

1094 New De Haven Street, Suite 100
West Conshohocken, PA 19428-2713
Info@buybooksontheweb.com
www.buybooksontheweb.com
Toll-free (877) BUY BOOK
Local Phone (610) 941-9999
Fax (610) 941-9959

Printed in the United States of America

Published October 2013

~Table of Contents~

Acknowledgments i

Section 1

Salon Careers, Descriptions, and Supplies

Chapter 1: Spark Your Passion in School 2
A Half-Million Job Openings 2
Selecting a Salon Profession 4
School and In-Salon Education 6

Chapter 2: Hair 11
Chapter 3: Wigs, Hairpieces and Extensions 16
Chapter 4: Skin Care Procedures, Estheticians, Facials,
and Body Treatments 19
Aromatherapy 22
Microdermabrasion 22
Glycolic Peels 22
Paraffin 23
Waxing 24
Body Wraps 24
Perming and Tinting Eyelashes 25
Laser Hair Removal and Electrolysis 26
Makeup Artist/Cosmetician 27
Tattooing/Permanent Makeup 28
Body Piercing 30
Chapter 5: Massage Therapy 31
Chapter 6: Nails 35
Chapter 7: Receptionist, Salon Coordinator,
and Manager 39
Chapter 8: Distributor Sales Consultant 42
Beauty Supply Sales Clerk 48

Section 2

Selecting a Great Salon to work in!

Chapter 9:   Can This Be Your Dream Career? 50
             Students, Forge Ahead! 51
Chapter 10: Adventures of the Job Search 54
             Fresh Out of School ... Where Do I Go? 54
             Selecting the best salon 55
             Compensation (Rent or Commission) 61
Chapter 11: Success in Time! 63
             Chain Salons 65
Chapter 12: Dress for Success 66
Chapter 13: Rev Up Your Résumé 69
             Approach the Salons of Your Choice 71
             A Fail-Safe Interview 72
Chapter 14: Wow, I Found a Fabulous Job! 75
             Setting Up Your Work Area 76
Chapter 15: Focus on Your Goals 78

Appendix A: Cosmetology Boards 81
Appendix B: Massage Boards 86
Appendix C: Résumé 90
Appendix D: Cover Letter for Résumé 91

~ACKNOWLEDGMENTS~

This book is a tribute to everyone who has taught me valuable lessons over the years. My sincere appreciation goes out to these individuals, and groups too numerous to mention.

I thank my parents for teaching me the value of hard work and for giving me the confidence of knowing I can accomplish anything I set my mind to. I am truly blessed with having such wonderful role models.

I thank Gloria Kuchinskas for being a mentor and editing my writing.

I thank Tammy Wallen for helping me with my preliminary editing and keeping me motivated.

I thank the National League of American Pen Women for helping me to become a writer.

I thank Creative Nail Design for the 12 years of training I received working for them. They always had outstanding speakers. I always looked forward to returning from our international training with an overloaded brain and more ideas than I could ever use. But I did my best to implement as many as possible!

I thank Ace Beauty Company/Beauty Alliance for all the sales meetings I attended. The educators, distributors and manufacturers created the final motivation to write these books. Matrix, Nioxin, Joico, Aquage, Framesi, ABBA, American Crew and Wayne Grund were very informative and inspirational. Working with all these companies along with CND gave me the privilege of working with the best of the best in the salon industry!

I thank all the clients, bosses, co-workers, employees, salon owners, students, and fellow salon professionals I have encountered over the years.

I thank Anita Kinsler for typing most of my notes. She was a real trooper struggling with the ones I wrote in the middle of the night in the dark!

I thank Alvis Cameron and Emily Mullings of HealthWise Therapeutic Massage for helping me gather facts and information in the massage field.

I thank Marian Rizzo, from the Ocala Star Banner, for sharing publishing information with me.

I thank my students who helped with proofreading and typing, especially Geri Paxton, Cindy Tucker and Tara Knight.

I thank Beth Mansbridge for professionally editing my writing.

Last, but not least, I thank Ray Hammond. He allowed me to bounce ideas off him and gave me a huge office in which to sprawl out in.

~Section 1~

Salon Careers, Descriptions, and Supplies

*"When we have our hair, nails and makeup done,
women can be in jeans and a T-shirt,
and still feel pretty."*

—Kim Stevens

1

Spark Your Passion in School

I started cutting hair when I was 9 years old. At 18, I was in cosmetology school where doing a trim on a client was a breeze. But my first shampoo and set almost put me into convulsions. While my client was sitting under the dryer, I became more and more nervous thinking about the comb-out. After my client's hair was dry, I took the rollers out and ran a brush through her hair a few times. She said, "Thank you, that's great!" I realized I'd gotten all worked up for nothing!

Once I experienced that moment of completion with my first comb-out, a huge smile came over my face. I was at peace with the world again. Things were a blast after that.

There are a half-million job openings in the beauty profession, or 2½ jobs are available for each graduate. The average salon income, including tips, is about **$18.50 per hour** in the United States, according to the NACCAS (National Accrediting Commission of Cosmetology Arts & Science). Since the average income is **over $38,000 per year**, there is money to be made in the beauty industry.

The most successful individuals in the salon industry implement the ideas I'm sharing with you here. The beauty industry is an enjoyable profession. You can meet another friend every hour. This is a relaxed, playful, and creative career. Jobs in the beauty salon industry are low in stress. Most people enjoy visiting beauty salons. You have the opportunity to show your creative side. The work is rewarding because you make your client happy and beautiful.

"I wish I knew then what I know now." I hope to make your learning process easier than mine by helping you understand how to take advantage of the numerous opportunities ahead of you and how to find them. In the series of books I have created, these philosophies are based on many trials and errors.

Learn from other's success that has helped so many other professionals prosper from for years. I want everyone to love the profession as much as I do. This and other books in the series address just about every career opportunity you could have in the beauty business. They will help you with any role you could play in a salon. So get out your highlighter and post-it notes to mark the pages important to you.

The most basic beauty professions and specialties are:

Hairdresser
Barber
Extensions
Wigs
Skin
Makeup Artist/Cosmetician
Permanent Makeup
Body Piercing/Tattooing
Electrolysis
Body Wraps
Massage Therapist
Nail Tech
Receptionist
Manager
Distributor Sales Consultant
Beauty Supply Sales Clerk

To group all these roles, I could use a fancy term like Professional Service Providers. Instead I'll be referring to all of these service professionals or technicians as "techs" for simplicity's sake.

Selecting a Salon Profession and the Training Involved for Each Service

If you aren't sure which part of the profession to be in, here are some key points about many of the careers to pick from. Facials, makeup, massages, and pedicures are normally preformed in a quiet room or area. The soft music and tranquility appeal to introverted techs who don't like busyness around them.

Working with hair and nails, receptionists, sales consultants, speakers, or educators traditionally have more interaction and talk with many people. If you enjoy social interaction, conversing, and telling stories and jokes, these are up your alley. It's easy to please people when providing services that fit your personality.

Nail tech training in most states requires 250-500 hours and about $200 for basic supplies to get started. Training for permanent makeup and electrolysis in most states is a very short program, less than a full week; but it requires expensive equipment. Supplies can cost between $400-$800 to start up.

Massage therapists and hairdressers require approximately 1,500-2,000 hours of training and an initial investment of $500-$800 to be equipped. They spend the majority of time on their feet and require manual dexterity (good with hands).

Hair and makeup techs must be able to communicate and demonstrate a desirable finished result. They are usually more creative and artistic.

A successful tech should be good with their hands, pleasant, tactful with clients, and have a genuine interest in people.

Understanding color is equally important in many of these jobs. When you and the client are discussing color, the most common thing they say is, "I want a color that goes with everything." That's when you have to determine what their "everything" is. Training in color analysis, like the *Color Me Beautiful* system, helps you understand a client's skin tone so you can make the best recommendation for her. If you

4

aren't sure, ask her what her favorite colors are. Ask, "What do you have in your closet?" Look at the lipstick she's wearing. More details on color analysis are covered in Book 2.

Working on clients, you'll perform many types of analyses on various parts of the body, depending on your license.

The basic training most all licensed salon professionals will receive involves general theory that consists of chemistry, anatomy, and the structure of the hair, nails, face and/or body. You will also learn treatment, sanitation, sterilization, salon safety, professional ethics, salesmanship, retailing, booking appointments, working with the public, phone etiquette, cleanliness, and your state's laws, rules and regulations. To get a general understanding of what a school curriculum may consist of, an example outline can be found under "Hair" in chapter 2. You'll learn how to analyze clients before performing services on the parts of the body you are licensed to work on.

Students' first experiences can make all the difference in their feelings of confidence. I try to find kind, patient clients for my students' first services or let them bring in someone they are at ease with. This can lessen the stress of a nervous beginning student.

OK, back on track with the original topic, buying supplies (yes, we sometimes get sidetracked!). Some workplaces will have the majority of the supplies you need, so your purchases will be minimal. The majority of the supplies needed for each profession are listed in the next chapters. It can be a great reference when you're about to set up in a shop. I also give more detail on what's involved in that career. I suggest that students only invest in the supplies they want for their own personal use. The place where you work may supply much of your equipment and products, especially if you're an employee.

The salon industry offers numerous ways to get started working. In most cases, you'll attend school or a course, or work for someone for free in an apprenticeship. You'll have to check in your state to see if apprenticeships are accepted. Without a license, some states will allow you to become a shampoo person to get experience in doing hair and getting to know clients. This is a great way to start building clientele before you even start working in your new career. Some states allow students to earn hours toward graduation by working in salons. A few salons offer advanced on-the-job training while you're getting paid. If you lack the confidence to start working on clients once you have graduated, this would be perfect for you. Take a little time to learn about as many opportunities as you can by talking to people in the profession.

School and In-Salon Education

Selecting a school or an apprenticeship should be done with care and preparation. Some states allow a student to learn on-location at a salon. A senior tech or salon owner helps you through the learning process with theory and hands-on services with clients, especially after graduation. Salons can be stronger in hands-on education while schools may be stronger in theory. It's a never-ending learning career, so it stays challenging.

You will not get paid in most apprenticeships. More likely, you will have to pay to learn and be a helper. Some salon owners see this as an opportunity to get free help. Do your homework to make sure the owner will be an effective mentor. As apprentices become more experienced, they should perform more tasks under supervision.

Choosing the best school or apprenticeship for yourself can help you succeed. Find an educational facility that will give you adequate theory, hands-on training, and the skills it takes to become successful. A school is expected to help you pass state boards or testing. Each state has different requirements for licenses. Most states require state boards for hair, massage, skin care, and nails. Some will be written only and some will be hands-on too. (The schools will know the requirements.) Preparing for state boards is usually the most difficult part of the educational process, especially if you let it. The rest is pretty easy. Testing is a reflection of what you do in school. If you know it there, you'll know it at state boards.

A school typically shows you basic approaches to learning the services along with theory to help you pass your tests. There is no law that state schools have to teach you specifically how to do each required service, but hopefully they will. I had a nail artist (as an instructor) hand me nail products and say, "Do a nail." It would not have been so bad if I had ever seen an artificial nail being put on. But back in 1982 (the Dark Ages), there really were not any "nail instructors." She didn't know she was supposed to say *something* to help us! Many things have changed since then. Schools will have full-time staff who only teach and part-time staff who also work in salons. Either way, a good instructor will want to excite, motivate and inspire you.

In some areas, your choice of schools may be limited. If you are fortunate to be in an area with many schools, investigate your options. If you aren't sure how to find schools in your state, a list of <u>State Boards for the Beauty Industry</u> can be found in Appendix A and <u>Massage</u> in Appendix B.

Often, people ask about the cost of attending my school. When they shop for schools merely by asking about prices, they don't understand the importance of quality or why an alarming 75% of students don't succeed in their fields. Sometimes it's worth a little more drive time or expense to benefit you in the long run.

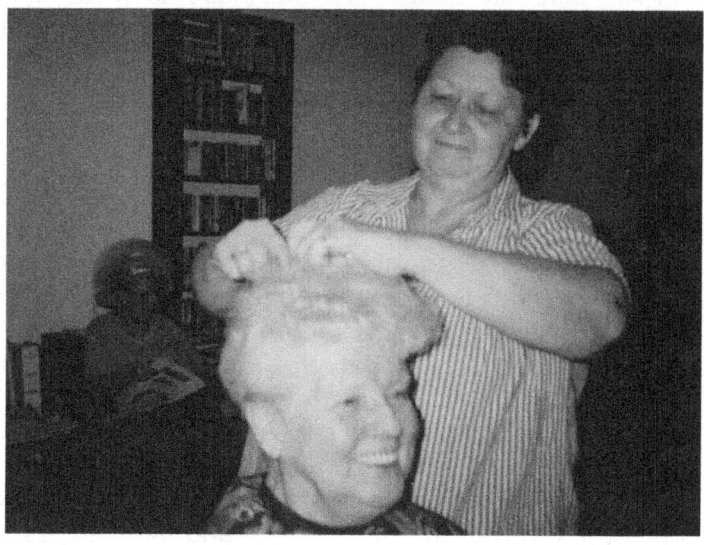

Lois Woerner (hairdresser since 1975) working on her client Bernice at her salon, Mane Styles, Ocala, FL

If you choose to work with hair, remember that by 2005, half the population will be over 50 years old, according to the U.S. Census Bureau. They have the time and money to spend on themselves. They want to look younger, feel better, and be healthier. Think gray coverage! This is doubly important to know, because hair coloring is one of the most profitable services offered in a salon. People over 50 pamper themselves or need therapy, such as massages. Keep retailing in mind too!

If you talk to others in the profession, they can cue you in on the most popular services for clients. Hopefully, while in school, you'll be exposed to many facets of the beauty business. Don't limit your training, because trends and styles return over time. We often lean toward specialties in this industry that can be fads. When I was checking out schools, one of my criteria was finding a cosmetology school that included artificial nails as part of its curriculum. In the early '80s, that was very difficult to find since it was still new. I did find a school willing to get a nail instructor, even though it took a little coaxing on my part.

Keep in mind that no one school will suit all your needs. While I was looking into schools, I found many which had mother-like instructors who told the students what to do—like they were her kids. Some students need that constant guidance and it fit many students' needs to keep them on track. I was very focused on trying everything I could get my hands on, so I was looking more for a school that had less nurturing and more "show me, then let me go do it." (The same will apply when searching for salons to work in.) So I was happy with my choice of school to fit my personality.

Your primary goal is to find one that is truly interested in your success. Then look at the other key points of interest. Most of your knowledge is gained from their experience and education. A good school with the proper instructor spells success.

Look at the student/instructor ratio. Once, while I was teaching a workshop at a community college, I noticed the classroom had forty-two students with just one instructor each night. Even with the most skilled and talented teacher, quality one-on-one training will be difficult with this ratio. Finding a talented instructor is a painstaking job, not just for students, but for schools as well. Instructors need the ability to interact with students, answer questions clearly, demonstrate processes, and inspire the students. Schools may bring in guest speakers to present new material that benefits both students and instructors.

Schools may supply many of your products, and you may be responsible for the more costly tools or equipment. Students sometimes elect to purchase their own products in order to better learn or have their desired supplies. Just remember to put your name on everything that's yours and take home or lock up your equipment.

Some schools will have a library and are pleased to allow the students free use. Use it to your advantage! I realize that many of us, especially "artists," may not particularly care to read, but look at it this way: For every page you read, you'll earn another five dollars a year in your career. Hmm ... how many pages have I written and read?

In chapters 2-8, you'll be given job descriptions, lists of items needed/wanted to get started, and information pertinent to that particular field.

Each state has different requirements for licensing or certification. Contact the cosmetology, massage, or health department in the capital city of your state (many are listed in the appendix of this book). Taking a state board may be required for licensing. If you are on a military base, your license should be good no matter where you are located.

For some of the professions, I list general requirements you need to attend school and become licensed. Make sure you have your license (or temporary license) displayed as soon as you start working.

Anthony Lizzo, 30 years experience, Tony's Salon, Ocala, FL

2 _____

Hair

*"I'm a hairdresser!
I cosmetically and psychologically transform
the images and destinies of fellow human
beings. What do you do?"*
                                        —Matrix T-shirt

A cosmetology course consists of haircutting, styling, coloring, perming, and an introduction to other services such as facial treatments, waxing, eyelash and brow tinting, makeup application, and nail services on hands and feet.

The curriculum for students enrolled in a cosmetology course could require anywhere from 1,000-3,500 hours of training depending upon which state you live in. The following is a job description for a hairdresser/barber and a possible school curriculum required by a typical state:

(a) 1,500-Hour Hair Course
History and fundamentals of cosmetology or barbering
Elementary chemistry relating to sterilization, sanitation,
  bacteriology, and hygiene
Implements
Shaving
Anatomy of the skin, scalp and hair

Haircutting, hairstyling, and blow-drying
Hairpieces
Chemical theory (permanent waving, hair coloring,
  bleaching and straightening)
Thermal reconditioning treatment and demineralizing
  treatment
Manicure, pedicure and artificial nails
Anatomy, physiology and systems structure of the head,
  face and neck, including muscles and nerves
Makeup, skin care and waxing
Theory of massage, facial treatment
Disorders of the skin, scalp and hair
Cosmetology or barber law, rules, and regulations
Business management and salesmanship
Preparation for seeking employment
Approximate Total Hours: 250

(b) Chemical Hours:
Permanent waving
Hair relaxing
Hair coloring, bleaching, touch-ups and toning
Manicures, pedicures and artificial nails
Approximate Total Hours: 350

(c) Physical Hours:
Shampooing and rinses
Hair care, scalp care and treatments
Haircutting
Shaving (beards and mustaches)
Hairpiece-fitting
Hairstyling and blow-drying
Facials, waxing, tweezing and makeup
Manicures, pedicures and artificial nails
Approximate Total Hours: 1,000-1,500

You may also learn finger waves, hot combs, comb-outs, reactions on hair, the chemistry of cold wave solutions, the chemistry of color, the color wheel, hair color removal, color correction, glazing, low lights, and chemical action of hair color. Updos, braiding, razor cuts, extensions, frosting, reverse frosting, cholesterol and scalp treatment with high frequency, body treatment, and equipment in the salon may also be part of the school's chosen curriculum.

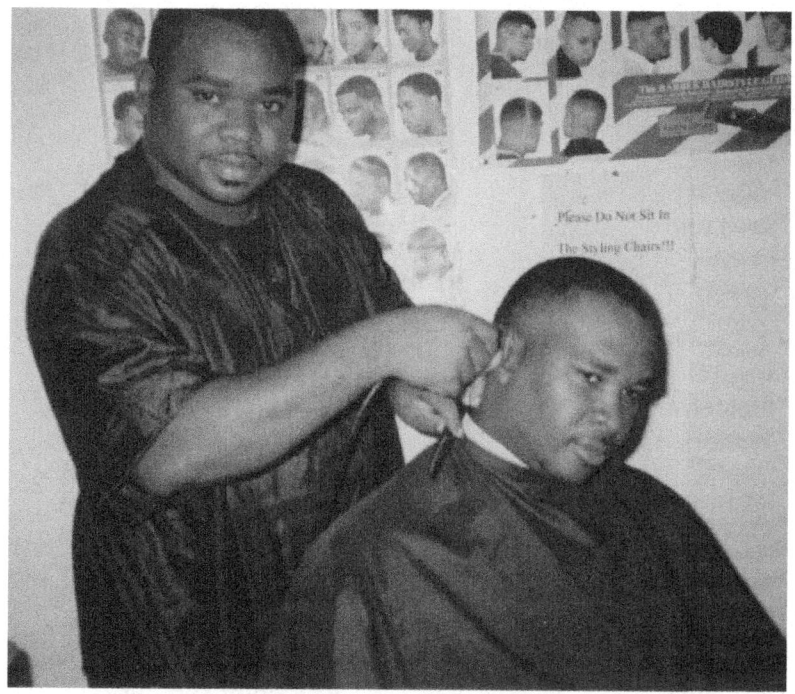

Rev. Dennis Hagins, shaving his brother Emmanuel Hagins at
Neu Beginin Total Salon, Ocala, FL

Barbershops usually don't take appointments; they strictly accept walk-ins on a first-come-first-serve basis. They do speedy in and out haircuts with very little retailing. Most states have barber licenses that are slightly different from cosmetology licenses. Even though they are trained to do chemical services like perms and coloring, they don't perform these as often as hairdressers do. Barbers do more volume and usually at a lower price.

A tip I've heard:
Never give yourself a haircut after three margaritas.

Following is a list of station supplies, back bar (at the shampoo bowl), dispensary (storage and mixing room), and retail supplies needed to do hair.

Supplies for Setting up a Station or Dispensary:

Hair station with mirror
Hydraulic chair
Sink
Hood dryer
Cabinet
Hand mirror
Hairstyling books
Dry sanitizer
Wet sanitizer
Gowns
Neck strips
Scissors or shears
Combs
Picks
Rollers
Brushes
Blow dryer
Diffuser
Barbicide
Ship-shape comb cleaner
Clean towel cabinet
Dirty towel hamper
Garbage can
Shampoo & cutting capes
Spray bottle
Bobby pins and hairpins
Perm rods
Perm papers
Perms
Perm treatments
Timer

Cotton
Straightener
Relaxer
Color chart
Hair color (and rack)
Developer
Key to roll tubes
Mixing bowls
Application brushes
Irons and hot combs
Clippers
Clipper oil
Powder
Razors
Shave cream
Application bottles
Gloves
Powder
Hair color remover
Stain remover for the skin
Bleach, on scalp
Bleach, off the scalp
Frosting caps
Foil papers
Dispensary scissors
Frosting hooks
Smock or apron
Rinses
Purple shampoo
Hair clips

<u>Back Bar and Retail:</u> These are supplies you will need at the shampoo bowl, hair station, and to sell:

Shampoos	Gels and styling lotions
Brushes	Foam or mousse
Conditioner	Straightening lotions
Curling irons	Finishing spray
Pumps	Working spray
Blow dryers	Pomades
Spray conditioner	Hand lotion
Diffuser	Rollers
Reconstructor	

Retail Display Case at Designerline, Ocala, FL

3

Wigs, Hairpieces and Extensions

Wigs come in an array of styles and are sold in many different locations. Wigs sell for fun and for cosmetic purposes, including for children. Hairpieces are needed for hair problems like thyroid or scalp conditions, brain surgery, alopecia (baldness in spots), or after cancer treatment. Older women lose hair mainly from hormone problems, men from pattern baldness.

Wigs and hairpieces come in short, medium, and long lengths. They are made with synthetic or human hair to create natural-looking wigs, perukes, periwigs, toupees, costume wigs, falls, extensions, accents, and eyelashes. Each type requires different services. Special training is needed to properly work with these to prevent tangling the hair. Synthetic hair cannot be colored. Human hair, preferred by most professionals, can be colored, permed, and styled like natural hair.

A plaster mold of the head is made to match texture, color, and size. Each strand of hair is woven into the base. Then it is cut (possibly colored or permed) and styled to look natural. Clients return to the salon for permanent bonding, fusion, medical adhesives, and skin testing. You must first understand how the human hair is processed for the hairpieces to fully understand how to maintain its natural appearance.

In order for hairpieces to last, they go through a process. Acid washes are performed on human hair to remove the cuticle. Synthetic hair must be reset by steam only. If procedures aren't followed properly, human and synthetic hair can be damaged. You can see the opportunities in a very specialized profession that can pay well. You may be trained to style wigs as an added service, or go deeper, into making them.

One woman had a few clients with extremely thin hair. She would get the clients two wiglets that were about the size of a woman's hand. She would wet or wash the hairpiece, set and dry it. When the client came into the shop, she inserted the prepared hair. The natural hair was parted and moved to the outside of the hairpiece, then bobby-pinned. It made the rest of their hair look thicker. She had of course removed the piece the client walked in with and it would be ready when the client returned the next week for her shampoo and set. The clients were so happy having thicker hair.

Extensions

Permanent hair extensions can give your clients a whole new look and change the way they feel about themselves. Anyone who has been in the business for a while has seen a client unhappy with her lack of hair. Whether it's a natural problem or a botched job, you can make thin or short hair thick and long. Gloria V. Johnson of Neu Beginin' Total Salon in Ocala, Florida, has shared with me how to create a highlighted look by introducing new colors or even different textures to hair for men and women. This service is for actors and actresses needing a new look and is extremely popular with African-American clients.

Extensions can be placed in several different ways:
- Sewn on (braiding natural hair and attaching commercial hair with thread)
- Weft (attach the weft to natural braided hair)
- Bonding (attach commercial hair with bonding glue to the scalp of natural hair)

17

- Latch hook (using a hook to attach commercial hair to the natural hair)
- Infusion (heat glue is applied to the commercial hair and to the natural hair)
- Braid method (attaching commercial hair by braiding hair to natural hair)
- Hidden stitch (using thread to connect the commercial hair to the natural hair)

Experienced stylists find extensions to be good moneymakers since many hairdressers charge double the hourly rate. It is the longest procedure done in a salon.

<u>Items Needed</u>:

Human or synthetic hair	Scissors
Adhesive	Hooks
Thermal guns	Bonding glue
Threads	Needles
Bobbin-holding machines	

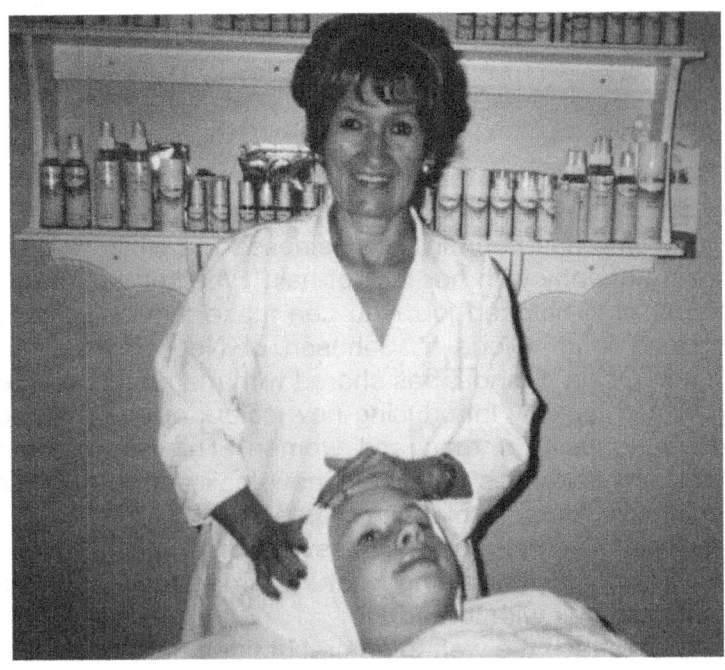

Maria Brown at Designerline in Ocala, FL
is preparing Crystal for a facial

4

Skin Care Procedures, Estheticians, Facials, and Body Treatments

Estheticians specialize in the esthetics or cleansing and beautifying of the skin. Facial treatments are designed to promote relaxation, to improve your skin's appearance, and for total skin health. As we age, care of the skin becomes critical. Fighting wrinkles and skin discoloration requires skin maintenance. Most clients' concerns are that of sun-damaged and prematurely aging skin. Many salons now offer a variety of spa-related services. By educating clients about skin care and introducing your clients to good skin-care products, you'll gain loyal spa clients.

The trained skin care specialist will customize the facial according to the client's needs. This will establish the basis of the products you'll recommend for home care maintenance. The average skin care specialist sells 100% of the service ticket. For example, if a client spends $50 for a facial, she will commonly purchase about $50 in skincare products for home use. Personalized programs with a variety of treatments can be designed to treat the whole body as well as the mind. Relaxing music and aromatherapy set the mood for a meditative state. You can set up a month-long regimen of treatments.

Aromatherapy can stimulate or relax a person depending on what scents are prescribed to appeal to the sense of smell. Acne or glycolic treatments will improve the appearance of the face. Detoxifying and nutritional supplements make the clients feel good from the inside. Then finish off with the basic skin care system they will want to establish for life.

Facial services may consist of the following:

Basic facials
European facials
Paraffin masks
Egg masks
Deep pore cleansing
Steaming
Extractions
Herb, enzyme or protein
  masks
Gentle exfoliation
Face, neck & shoulder
  massage
Anti-aging treatment
Eye treatments
Rebalancing the skin
Antioxidants
Essential oils
Body polish
Luxurious moisturizing

Mud stimulation
Invigorating salt scrub
Calming essential oils
Waxing
Makeup
Color analysis
Hypnotherapy
Aromatherapy
Nutritional counseling
Exfoliation treatment
Alpha-hydroxy treatments
Deep pore cleansing
Glycolic acid peels
Microdermabrasion
Buffing
Body wraps
Detoxifying
body treatments

Items Desired for Facials:

Facial room (quiet area)
Low light or dimmer
Free of telephones & talk
Soft music
Facial chair
Client card
Sink or water
Warm water bowl
Bowl for mixing products

Steamer
Cotton
Sponges & chamois
Towels
Wash cloths
Headband
Hair cover
Towel wrap
Robe

Sheets
Blanket
Product line
Sales material
Retail shelf
Cleanser
Eye pads
Moisturizer
Eye cream
Toner
Astringent
Massage cream
Glycolic acid
Acne treatment
European facials
Towel warmer or
  microwave oven
Trash containers
Makeup mirrors
Brushes
Back treatment
Eye treatment
Mask

Peels
Scrub
Toner
Lip treatment
Skin plumping cream
Paraffin
Paraffin mask
Fan brush to apply
  paraffin
Tweezers
Vacuum and electric
  system
Galvanics
High frequency
Gloves for extractions
Brow-tinting materials
Body treatments
Body wrap supplies
Waxing supplies
Extraction tools
Treatments
Skin exfoliation materials

Applicator sticks (also used to remove products from jars)
Extractions, aromatherapy, or serums added to treatments
Color analysis materials with book of swatches
High-frequency treatments for face or scalp
Makeup material for costumes or the theater

Makeup and Retail Products:
Cleansers
Toners
Moisturizers
Eye creams or treatments
Acne treatment
Mask
Products to retard hair
  growth

Defoliators
Sunscreen
Makeup
Color swatches
Aromatherapy materials
Nutritional supplements
Body treatments
Glycolic treatments

Some states now require facials to be done with gloves. You may want to mention this in the client consultation. Note: Some people are allergic to latex. Non-latex and no-powder rubber gloves are available. When booking appointments, ask clients not to wear contact lenses during the service.

Aromatherapy

Aromatherapy uses extracts from aromatic plants to calm nerves, stimulate thinking, get you in a desired mood, or even treat ailments. Extracts may come from flowers, herbs, leaves, bark, or rind from plants. The body absorbs oils through the skin with direct application, inhaled from candles, or added to bath water.

Microdermabrasion

This procedure is used to resurface the skin in addition to chemical peels. (Dermabrasion is a deeper chemical peel). It is designed to reduce skin disorders or acne, and the signs of aging or sun-damaged skin. It softens fine lines and brown spots. Dead cells on the surface of the skin and oily plugs in pores are removed with a machine. An abrasive material of aluminum oxide crystals is deposited on the skin surface under pressure, similar to mild sandblasting, and then the dead skin is suctioned off. Layers of the epidermis, or outer layer of the skin, are removed. The skin may feel tight and sunburned. It may also peel or have some redness or swelling depending on the depth of the treatment. In most cases, the skin appears flushed and feels soft and smooth.

Generally, six treatments performed two weeks apart are recommended. Normal activities can be resumed immediately. Some people use microdermabrasion along with alpha-hydroxy acid treatments. It is important for clients to protect their skin by following your professional retail recommendations.

Glycolic Peels

Peels are used to reduce wrinkling associated with sun damage, acne scars, blemishes, and areas of uneven skin pigmentation. A series of glycolic peels is intended to reduce fine lines and make the skin smoother and more uniform in color. These treatments are not as deep as dermabrasions, so the client doesn't need to hide for a day or two. Again, a professional retail regimen is recommended for best results.

Paraffin

Paraffin is a translucent, waxy mixture in which hands and feet are dipped, or which is brushed on the face or other parts of the body. The oils in the warm wax paraffin are absorbed into the skin, nails, and cuticle to relieve dryness, make hands softer and look more youthful. Paraffin is an excellent treatment each month, with the results lasting for days.

For clients with arthritis, a treatment once a week is recommended. The warmth of the wax loosens the crystallized synovial fluids. This lessens the pain for the clients and allows for better movement.

Supplies Needed:

Wax in the warmer	Booties
Lotion	Paintbrushes
Baggies	Gauze mask
Mitts	

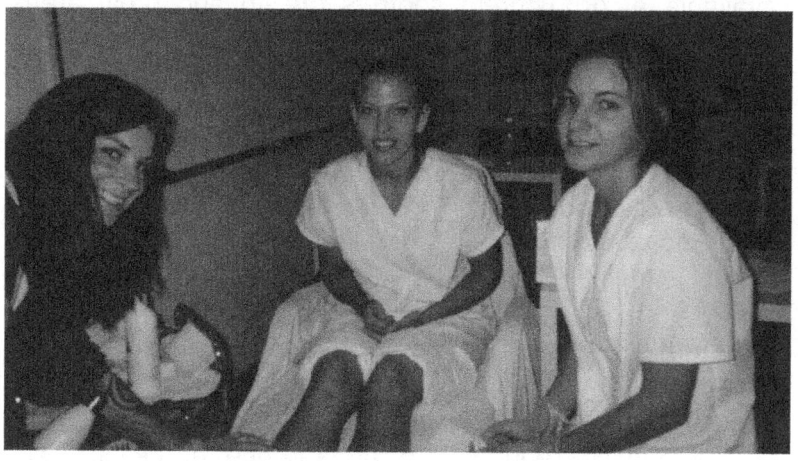

Three skin care student are practicing waxing techniques at Central Florida Community College. (Left to right), Kristen Scavo, Lauren Brockway-Keeley, and Heather Davis.

23

Waxing

Waxing is a high-profit service for temporary removal of unwanted hair from eyebrows, lips, sideburns, cheeks, chin, feet, toes, chest, back, arms, the nape, underarms, half legs, full legs, and for bikini areas. Clients can choose a salon that has an esthetician who offers waxing as a regular service in a treatment room.

Some salons have facial wax at the shampoo bowl applied by hairdressers. Some techs specialize in waxing in a facial room with a complete setup to remove hair for three to six weeks at a time. The benefits of waxing are that the hair, over time, gets softer and finer and less and less of it returns. Tweezing eyebrows and stray hairs around the chin area is another service clients may ask for.

Before the procedure, clients should not shave for at least 10 to 14 days. There should be no shaving between waxing appointments or the hair will continue to grow quickly and look thick. Clients should avoid the sun for 24 hours prior to waxing. Even a mild burn can make the skin more sensitive. No topical medications or moisturizers with alpha-hydroxy acids should be applied to the area to be waxed.

After waxing, remove excess wax with a gentle rub of milky lotion or baby oil. A lotion with 1% hydrocortisone (available at drugstores) soothes the lip and brow areas. The sun should be avoided for 24 to 48 hours after waxing. A loofah should be used on the legs and bikini area between waxing to prevent ingrown hairs.

Items Needed:

Wax in heated pot	Hydrocortisone
Hair removal strips,	Powder
large & small	Cooling lotion
Scissors	Wax cleaner
Preparation lotion	Tweezers

Body Wraps

This service reduces the appearance of cellulite and takes off inches. Some people believe body wraps just make people lose water weight. If you're trying to lose weight with proper diet and exercise, this can enhance your achievement. There are many kits on the professional market that contain most of the products needed. Each company will have its own application method, which requires training by the manufacturer's educator.

Perming and Tinting Eyelashes

These services are for people who spend a lot of time outdoors and have problems with makeup smearing. It is helpful for those who have trouble with their eyesight or applying makeup. There is also the convenience of not having to apply as much makeup each day. Perming eyelashes is very much like perming hair—but in miniature. It takes a steady hand. When lashes are curled and darkened, they look longer and thicker.

In the process, a gel adhesive is placed on the eyelids and at the base of the lashes. The lashes are placed on tiny perming rods made of flexible foam. Perming solution is daubed on and then followed by a neutralizer. These processes have kits with most of the ingredients needed. Note that latex may be in eyelash adhesives. A skin patch test should be performed 24 hours before application. The service lasts about 3 months. The perming kit is about $60 for two dozen applications. The price for perming averages $48.

Tinting the lashes involves daubing the color on the lashes or the eyebrows (without getting it on the skin). It is similar to coloring the hair or eyebrows with hair color. But the colors do not need to be mixed; the color is ready to apply from the bottle. It adds darker hues to eyebrows and lashes. The tint kit is about $50 and has about four dozen applications. The service lasts about 3 months. The price for tinting is $20. You can see how these services can be very profitable!

Because you're working in the eye area, you need to be sure of each step you perform. Some states will require a cosmetology or esthetician license to perform these services, so check with your state board.

Laser Hair Removal and Electrolysis

Laser hair removal is a noninvasive method to disable the hair structure without damaging the surrounding skin. A cool gel is applied to the skin and then a laser is passed over the coated area. The only sensation most people feel is the gel. Application of enough heat to the base of the hair follicle destroys all the cells that cause the hair to grow.

Electrolysis hair removal is done with a needle or probe that is inserted into the opening of the follicle. Then an electrical current is passed through the hair follicle, which destroys the hair growth. Another method is using tweezers to grasp the hair and send an electrical current into the hair follicle. These methods of permanently removing unwanted hair are virtually painless.

It takes an average of 6 to 12 weeks for hair to grow in cycles. The best time to treat it is when the hair grows out. A series of treatments is needed since a small percentage of re-growth with finer hairs is possible. If the insertion is done correctly and the right amount of heat is applied, the hair will not grow back. Electrolysis is the most effective way to completely and permanently remove unwanted hair. The average cost is at least $1 a minute.

Retail Makeup Area

Makeup Artist/Cosmetician
How many tubes of lipstick are in your purse right now?

Makeup artists prepare the skin and apply makeup to the face. (To apply the makeup, the skin needs to be prepped or the makeup will not go on smoothly.) Makeup artists teach customers how to apply and remove makeup and choose the right colors. They apply makeup for brides, customers on special occasions, photographic models, actors, pageant participants, and television actors. They may work in a salon or department store. Some may work for doctors doing facials, helping skin cancer patients, or doing makeup for reconstruction. Others will be involved with the theater or in weddings, and even funerals.

More advanced makeup artists may chose a different canvas to work on, the human body. To get into stage productions that allow these artists to change actors' appearances, one needs to have a great eye for color, shape and form. They can make actors look 20 years younger, 20 years older, give them scars, gashing wounds, mustaches, and prosthetics or change their look altogether.

Makeup artists may have other titles depending upon where they work, such as cosmetician, beauty consultant or cosmetic consultant. Trained sales consultants represent one or more lines of cosmetics in drugstores, department stores or salons. They are expected to produce high volumes of sales by promoting the beauty products.

Makeup Supplies and Retail Materials: Recommended items for makeup application that may also be retailed:

Eye makeup remover	Brow brush
Cleanser	Blush
Toner	Eye shadow
Moisturizer (for dry & oily skin)	Lipstick
	Lip liner
Foundation	Lip brush
Powder	Eyeliner brush
Contour powder	Eyeliner
Eyebrow pencils	Concealer
Eyebrow powder	Mascara

Mascara applicator
Brow brush
Makeup brushes
Tweezers
Mirror
Counter
Lights
Alcohol
Tissues
Cotton swabs
Applicator brushes &
  sponges
Toothpicks for adhesive &
  eyelash tint

Headbands, disposable or
  machine washable
Camera (Polaroid) for
  makeovers
Sharpener
Eyelash curler
Hair clips
Drape cloth
Artificial lashes
Adhesive
Eyelash tint
Disposable gloves

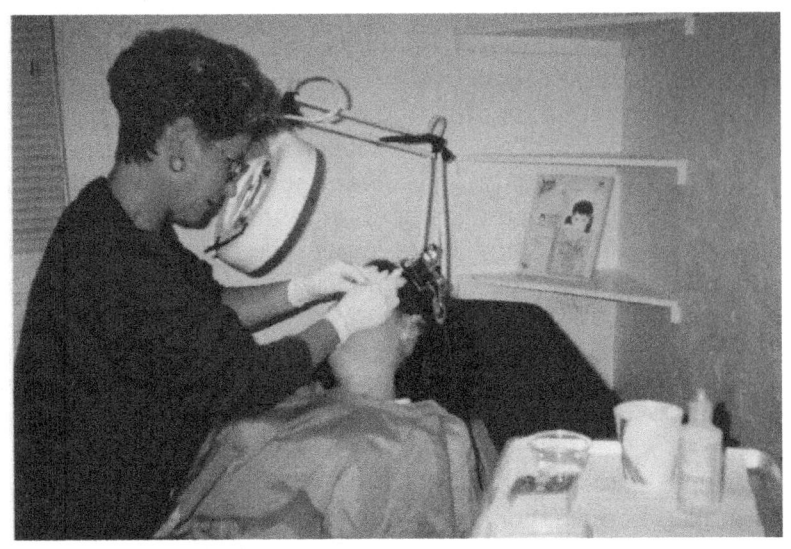

Kathie Dudley, Kathie's Permanent Makeup, Ocala, FL

Tattooing/Permanent Makeup

Tattooing involves implantation of pigment into the dermal layers of the skin. Tattoo artists use an electrically powered, vertical-vibrating instrument to inject the tattoo pigment 50 to 3,000 times per minute into the skin. Tattooing and body piercing have been used by many cultures, some dating back to at least 2000 B.C.

For the most part, there is not any special technical licensing for piercers or tattoo artists. In some states with no regulation, local cities set up their own standards. In some states, the state does license piercers, but this is largely a health board license, which ensures studios adhere to a set of rules governing use of an autoclave and sterile procedures.

In some areas, a doctor's inspection and recommendation are required for an annual application and license. There are courses you can take, apprenticeships, and diplomas available to show you have attended a course or ordered it through a magazine. Scary if you're a client, huh? But experience is the real teacher under an established, knowledgeable tech.

Permanent makeup can change the color and the shape of your lips, enhance the hairline and save time from daily makeup application. Eyebrows and eyelashes can appear fuller, scars camouflaged, areolas restored after a mastectomy, as well as making stretch marks, birthmarks, freckles, and age spots less noticeable. A wide variety of colors and techniques are used on men and women to hide flaws or aid people. Some people are allergic to makeup, have trouble with it smearing or have difficulties applying makeup. Anesthetics are applied by PMU (permanent makeup) techs to minimize the pain before tattooing the specific parts of the body. Refer to: http://www.permanentmakeupsociety.com/

Items Needed:

Tattoo machine	Sharp needle disposal
Power supply	containers
Foot pedal & cord	Tray to work from
Needles, bars & tubes	Chairs for client and artist
Pigment & palette	Light
Topical treatments	Consent forms
Medical sanitizing agents	Catalogs and posters
Gloves	

Body Piercers: Chris Collins, owner of Fat Kats, Ocala, FL
and Daniel Ghigliotty.

Body Piercing

This is the art of piercing or placing a hole in the skin to insert jewelry in such places as the ear, nose, navel, eyebrow, lip and tongue (the most popular visible areas to pierce). It is popular with some young adults. There are a variety of metals used, such as titanium, niobium, 14-karat gold (for ears), and surgical steel (the most used) to make studs, banana bells, barbells and bars. For most body parts, a hollow needle is passed through the skin, then the jewelry follows. A little bleeding or swelling may result.

One certification that a very small number of studios have is an *Old Gauntlet Master Piercer* and similar certificates. These are quite meaningful because they indicate multiple years of piercing.

5

Massage Therapy

"Heaven" is a hot oil scalp massage treatment along with a peppermint foot massage. Massage is defined as the systematic manual or mechanical manipulation of the soft tissues of the body for the purpose of promoting circulation of the blood and lymph, and relaxation affecting the muscles, organs, myofasciae, tendons, ligaments, and fasciae.

Massage is also extremely effective and beneficial in treating chronic pain, improving organ function, elevating cellular activity, enhancing muscle tone, increasing lymphatic circulation, relieving stress, and aiding the digestion and absorption of nutrients. The proven medical benefits have tremendous positive physiological effects.

According to Dr. Hans Gruenn, M.D., close to 90% of visits to primary care physicians are for stress-related conditions. The Florida State Massage Therapy Association lists what conditions can be helped through massage: body pain, tendonitis, bursitis, pinched nerves, arthritis (noninflammatory), constipation, extremity numbness, insomnia, eyestrain, poor concentration, depression, anxiety, ulcers, irritability, anger, high blood pressure, heart disease, neuritis, poor circulation, physical and emotional exhaustion.

Massage services can enhance a person's mental state as well as aid in the body healing itself. It lessens the severity of numerous problems like pain, stress, migraines, neurological damage, diabetes, asthma, autism, hyperactivity, anxiety, Alzheimer's, unbalanced hormones, digestive problems, while strengthening the immune system, increasing circulation, lessening toxins in the body, and boosting athletic performance. Massage flushes toxins such as lactic acid out of the muscles. Since muscles are composed of greater than 75% water, the active massage creates a pumping effect to purge latent toxins. Massage is to be used in conjunction with drinking large amounts of water. Many insurance companies are covering massage for certain conditions and disorders.

To help patients with stress and pain, doctors often prescribe massage. It is also a part of physical therapy, sports medicine, and some nursing practices. The average client visits a trained massage therapist about 7 times a year.

"If you have a massage every week,
You will have 2/3 fewer illnesses."
—Hans Gruenn, M.D., Los Angeles, CA

Massage can be effective in lowering stress and anxiety. A massage therapy clinic can be a body shop as well as an inner health clinic. It's common for a client to break down and cry while you're working on them. For some people, this is the most they have been touched by someone in ages, even if they have a mate.

Each state requires a different education. The American Massage Therapy Association and The National Certification Board can give you details of the requirements you need in your state.

It takes time to build a steady clientele. Massage therapists often work with hospices, state agencies, doctors and chiropractors. One way to get some business quickly is to go to places where you'll find many people, like a plant, large company, airport, mall or conventions, and offer 5-minute chair massages for $5. Though $1 per minute is common, you can give better prices for longer periods of time, like $13 for 15 minutes and $25 for 30 minutes. If you're working in a salon or a location where you need to build up your own business, you can offer a short free or reduced service for the first time to get clients hooked.

The nice thing about massage is the low cost of supplies to maintain. Once you obtain your table and linens, the lotion and sanitizer will be the main items you'll need to restock. Once massage therapists get established, they often can add extras for their clients.

Nutritional supplements are often recommended by massage therapists for nutritional healing. A great resource is the book *Prescription for Nutritional Healing: A Practical A-Z Reference to Drug-Free Remedies Using Vitamins, Minerals, Herbs, and Food Supplements, (Prescription for Nutritional Healing, 3rd Ed.)* by James F. Balch, M.D., and Phyllis A. Balch, CNC.

Here is a list of extra services you can offer.

Services Offered by a Massage Therapist:

Sports massage
Neuromuscular therapy
Swedish massage
Pregnancy massage
Infant massage
Craniosacral
   accupressure
Shiatsu
Rolfing
Trager
Structural integration
Orthobionomy
Myofascial release
Hydrotherapy
Reflexology
Manual lymphatic
   drainage
Polarity
Spa techniques
Hot compresses
Body facials
Body wraps
Seaweed wraps
Mud masks
Aromatherapy
Nutritional supplements
Holistic treatments
Colonics
Body treatments
Exfoliation

Reflexology

Reflexology employs the principle that glands, organs and various parts of the body have reflex areas that respond from pressure to the hands and feet. This stress-releasing technique preformed by hand, like massage, has been around since ancient civilization.

It seems that almost all cultures used some form of foot treatment as part of their health practices. It is believed that over 7,000 nerves in the feet correspond to every muscle system or organ in the body. If a client has a tender spot on the foot, it may be an indication of a problem area in the body. Diagrams are helpful for people to see reflex points mapped out, since massage therapists are not supposed to diagnose people.

Most massage experts agree this service helps allow the body's natural ability to heal itself by creating balance throughout the entire body. Some people who are ticklish feel they cannot get a pedicure or foot massage. But with firm pressure, it is actually extremely relaxing. Some clients will even fall asleep.

Items Needed:

Quiet room	Towels
Massage table	Fan
Lotion or oil	Heater and air
Sheet, drapes &	conditioning, if available
pillowcases	Aromatherapy candles &
Sanitizer	essential oils
Music	Hydrocollator (hot packs)
Pillows for neck &	Cold packs
under legs	Bolsters
Face cradle covers	

Massage Items to Sell:

Aromatherapy candles	Roller beads
Essential oils	Magnets
Nutritional supplements	Fragrant bath sachets
Vibrating devices	Body lotion

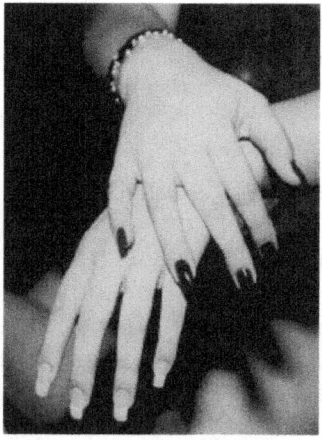

Winning competition nails created by Lynn in Orlando, FL

6

Nails

Nail artists can transform plain-looking hands to something more elegant with nail extensions and therapeutic treatments. Artificial nails are becoming more and more popular, even on toes. You create a 3-D sculpture using a brush and files, then paint your work. So some artistry, including any kind of arts and crafts in your background, is a plus.

Most women cannot grow their own long nails. The thing I hear most is that they think something is wrong with them since their nails don't grow. They think they lack calcium or have some deficiency. The truth is, most of us know one or two women who can grow their own long nails. I tell my clients, "Those women are unusual, and you are perfectly normal."

Let's face it, this is why we stay in business.

"Go into the bathroom and undo your pants."
(You can imagine the client's response ...)
"No, don't come out with them undone!"
                                        —*Jessica Nippers, Nail Tech*

This is how Jessica finds out if the client's nails will be too long for comfort. Not only do women enjoy their nails, but the person getting their back scratched enjoys them too. This is probably the easiest of the services for customer satisfaction. When someone who has never been able to grow her own nails, walks into a salon and walks out with long nails, she *is* happy. Years ago, it didn't even matter how thick or how bad they looked, just as long as they were long!

Today, women are becoming more and more savvy on the looks of the nails. After someone has had a great nail service, they won't be happy with mediocre work. So the market is weeding out the unskilled techs.

Most anyone with a desire to learn, the right education and a qualified instructor can learn to apply a set of nails. If you have the opportunity to find a skilled instructor, feel blessed. Many schools have hairdressers teaching nail services or someone who couldn't make any money doing nails as the teacher. This is usually the most difficult instructor for schools to find. It really takes a gift for someone to sit and teach a student the art of putting on a beautiful, long-lasting nail extension. In Florida, doing fill-ins isn't even a required service in which to become licensed, yet it is 80-90% of most established nail techs' services.

"Proper chemical matching" is one of the most crucial pieces of advice I give to people in the nail profession. Mixing different liquid and powder "systems" is what creates most of the problems nail techs experience. When you use all the recommended supplies in the line that are specifically designed to blend together, it ensures success. When you use the correct items, your biggest problems go away. It cannot be overemphasized that when nail techs use the chemical components that are designed for a one-on-one match up, the customer's nails are in no risk of chemical destruction.

The next crucial part of being a great nail tech is being educated within that product line. Since every product line varies greatly in the method of application, you'll need to fully understand that process. A *good* tech becomes *great* when she understands more about the products she uses.

Educating clients is a benefit too. When they are told about the process and the products, they tell their friends about featured items they recall. It impresses the people they tell, who want to try it too.

Make the nails as short as the client will let you at first. A quarter-inch more length on a nail may not seem like a lot, but it can get in the client's way and result in clients not returning. This is not a necessary service like haircuts, so follow-up calls can help build your clientele. I tell clients "two weeks is "maintenance time" and "three weeks is repair time."

When you're a nail student or artist, you'll be sitting face-to-face with people while holding their hands. You get to know them so much more intimately than you do in most other services. They'll tell you things they haven't even told their own family, and you'll be wise to keep this information confidential.

Most of your clients will be female. If you want to attract more male clients, come up with different names that sound manly, such as "Men's Hand (or Foot) Treatment."

If you start out by charging discounted prices, you'll get more clients at first, but they are usually not long-term clients. If your skills are fairly good, you have a warm personality, you converse well with others, and you work in a high-end salon, you'll build more long-term clients.

List of Services:
Manicures - includes spa and hot oil
Pedicures - may include toenail overlay
Extensions - sculptured nails, tips and/or gels
Nail wraps - silk, fiberglass and linen
Overlays (powder & liquid, gel, silk, fiberglass)
Party nails (tips, glue and polish for temporary service)
Extension removal - soak product off with acetone
Glycolic or exfoliation treatment for hands and feet

Fill-ins or rebalancing
Repairs
Buff & polish
Polish change

Nail Supplies:
Table
Chair
Lamp with bulb
Garbage can
Towels
Paper towels
Nail polish
Base coat
Top coat
Nail polish remover
Cotton
Files
Buffer
Nail cutters
Nippers
Nail sanitizer
Primer
Tips
Adhesive
Forms
Liquid
Powder

Items for Retailing:
Nail polish
Nail polish remover
Files
Buffer
Nail cutters
Nippers
Adhesive for repairs
Repair kit
Cuticle oil
Hand lotion
Base coat

French manicure
Nail art
Airbrushing
Paraffin treatment

Brush
Brush for cleaning
Silk
Fiberglass
Acetone or product
 remover
Hand sanitizer
Disinfectant and holder
Alcohol
Cuticle oil
Hand lotion
Finger bowl
Cuticle remover
Orangewood sticks
Footbath
Disinfectant
Sloughing lotion or
 exfoliator
Callous scraper
Toenail clippers
Toe dividers
Paper shoes or flip-flops

Top coat
Cuticle remover
Orangewood sticks
Sloughing lotion
Callous scraper
Pumice stone
Toe dividers
Nail polish dryers
Jewelry
Nail charms
Decals

Robbe Lankford, Salon Coordinator at Scissorhands,
Ocala, FL

7

Receptionist, Salon Coordinator, and Manager

A creative, thinking coordinator with good verbal communication skills in the workplace is like the beautiful accessories that go with a plain black dress. She creates style, excitement and a flow to the entire salon. How you dress, talk and act can change the way others see you and also influence the way you see yourself. If you want to work in an atmosphere where you dress extravagantly and feel as if you're at a party hobnobbing with socialites, this is the place to be.

Business owners and managers typically spend their days running the business. Salon owners spend most of their days working on clients. A great coordinator improves the entire salon because she can oversee everything that's going on and tend to clients. In many cases she will eventually run the place. The coordinator will not only understand each tech's specialties and desires, but also deal with clutter that invades the place. A salon without a coordinator looks very different after seven hours of techs continuously working on clients. She will keep the place looking neat and organized.

The coordinator needs to focus on the customers first. As a coordinator/manager, you need to wear many hats: manager, hostess, secretary, personal director, problem solver, ambassador, peacemaker, team motivator, file maintainer, and records and book keeper. You need to have some understanding of all salon procedures, and products to be retailed with them. Your ability to promote specials and retail products, present new items, and create new business for the salon makes you very valuable to the salon.

Since clients are calling and coming into the salon, they are looking for new things! Your telephone skills involve screening calls to get the information you need without upsetting the caller, taking messages, and occasionally dealing with difficult callers and public encounters. You should have instinctual ways to build rapport quickly and easily with strangers. You are the heartbeat of the shop. You'll be the key person who keeps it running smoothly and steadily.

Don't hesitate to bring any problems to management's attention. Your perks for working in a salon are usually a fun, happy work environment and free (or reduced) salon services during your off-time.

Coordinator's Duties:
- Greet clients by name and introduce them to their techs.
- Sell and educate on salon services over the phone.
- Book appointments. On the phone, be sure to repeat the day, date, and time.
- Maintain a good attitude, especially with customers.

- Dress professionally; keep your hair styled and nails neatly manicured. Clients see yours first.
- Close retail sales.
- To prevent "no-shows" among new clients, put a star (*) to show that person needs to be called. For example: "This is Salon A calling to confirm your appointment at one o'clock today." ... "Thank you, good-bye."
- Take names and numbers of people you cannot fit in at the time they prefer. In case of cancellations, you can fit them in.
- Make sure each technician has her schedule marked in the appointment book.
- Perform bookkeeping duties daily and ensure the staff turns in their money.
- Straighten retail sales areas once or twice a week as needed.
- Keep tabs on the inventory and paper supplies, and order before inventory runs out.
- Go to the store two or three times a month to get supplies.
- Keep the shop neat and organized.
- Once a week, go through the magazines, water the plants, and straighten the back rooms.
- Keep the desk clean and organized.
- Straighten the bathroom, coffee area, and reception area daily.
- Empty the garbage.
- Put the clean towels away.
- Check with the management for daily tasks that may need to be completed.

8

Distributor Sales Consultant

A distributor sales consultant calls upon salons, takes orders, sometimes delivers orders, explains new products, and tells what is on sale. They aren't always hairdressers or people who have been in the beauty industry, but people who are good with "selling."

When a distributor sales consultant first starts, some distributors will hold your hand through the learning process and others will expect you to figure things out on your own. Some will pay commissions, some a salary, and some will pay both. They all have advantages and disadvantages. When you're first starting in sales in a brand new territory (salons not using your products), it will take time to establish new business. You can't get discouraged easily if you are to succeed. If you're a great salesperson and you step into someone else's established territory, it should only be a matter of time to get acquainted with the routine.

The sales manager will be the one who will usually train you the most. For a while, new reps aren't expected to know everything about every product. Get your hands on old sales fliers and manuals for some fast education. If you don't know how to answer a question, be honest with your customer.

Look for a knowledgeable person within the distributorship as a support person to help you.

If you like to work independently and enjoy quite a bit of drive time, you will enjoy salon sales. I personally was bored with half my days alone in the car. I enjoy the interaction with people all day, so I went back to the salon full-time.

To be more successful with sales, be there consistently for the customers, take your job very seriously, study the information presented to you, and believe in total customer satisfaction.

Customers enjoy a monthly newsletter from the consultant. Take notes at the sales meetings and write down all the information on new products, special deals, and helpful tips for the newsletter. Include salons looking for techs and people looking to sell or buy salon equipment. Cover the issues considered important from a salon owner's point of view.

Write a statement about what your responsibilities are as their DSC. Explain the responsibilities of the warehouse, the salespeople on the phones, deliverymen, and the accounting department. Techs appreciate knowing whom to contact for their problems.

A big part of being a DSC is problem-solving. Often when customers call, it is about a problem. If they have a problem, do your best to listen and come up with a solution to make them happy.

"Fix the Problem and Not the Blame." When a customer does call with a problem, don't be concerned about whom to blame it on. That only fuels the fire. Thinking on your feet is very beneficial when dealing with a client. They may want to have a credit on their account or need an item ASAP. When in doubt, ask them. Let the client know you understand why they are upset with that specific problem. Then let them know what you can do about it. If you listen carefully, the client may have a solution within the complaint. When you apologize to the customer for the problem, say it sincerely. Even on the phone, your body language and gestures come across. Sometimes clients don't even need a solution; acknowledging their problem is enough.

If an order was short an item, your adding a few extra items to the missing product will satisfy them even more.

Sales consultants always enjoy customers who are organized enough to have a list ready and who can survive if something they ordered doesn't arrive. Others act as if their salon would cease to exist if they didn't receive one bottle of something immediately. Salons that are prepared with a list when the DSC arrives make it easier. In your salon, keep an eraser board or a running list so you don't forget anything. The sales consultant can then copy from it. Put a line through the items ordered so it can be erased when the order comes in.

Selling has its ups and downs. But a great salesperson will not be discouraged. The next door you walk into may create your biggest day ever. One year in our area, we had quite a few sales consultants. When Kim Cook first came into my salon as a DSC, he introduced himself and then proceeded to tell me "he was not going anywhere." Wow—he already told me something I wanted to hear! He told me he had over 20 years' experience as a distributor sales consultant and planned on sticking around. I instantly liked him! He seemed persistent and confident without being arrogant.

He was consistent with his visits, always walked in with some kind words and a smile on his face. He would show up the same time every other week. He was familiar with the entire product lines and the prices of top items. He could make recommendations, and he would follow through with problems and requests. He would sit and wait when he came in if he found I was busy doing three things at once. He usually had something in his hand when he walked in; he had literature, samples or something new to show me. When I asked questions, he usually had the technical understanding of the products to explain what I needed to know.

After a few years, he was transferring to a territory closer to home and I wanted to try my hand at sales. So, I know how walking into a new salon can be very unnerving, since I took over from him. When I first went into sales, I accompanied Kim to some of the salons. I rode with him for a week so I could have a better understanding of what I was to do. I had looked forward to seeing him come into my salon every two weeks and tried to continue in his role.

The customers liked the fact that another Kim was taking over, and there were no problems with remembering my name. He still worked within the company and I saw him regularly at our meetings. He was my mentor and coach. I wanted to develop professional relationships with the customers like he did.

First, I had to show my enthusiasm. Each week, I tried to walk in with something useful. The warehouse had all sorts of goodies I collected for my customers. I handed out video tapes, flyers (old ones with good information on products for new customers), price lists, sample products (especially good to walk into a new salon with), color charts, product descriptions, window decals, current sales sheets, the names and numbers of hotlines and anything else I could get my hands on. The fact that I took time to gather these items for them was greatly appreciated by my salons.

I informed those who didn't know me about my salon background. Many knew of me because of my nail business. But most didn't know I was an experienced hairdresser and skincare specialist. Finding a common factor when talking to people helps break the ice.

This is where verbal skills are important. Intelligent explanations are important when it comes to colorfully describing something new you want your clients to try. Your honesty in communication, and understanding how to read people are a must. When you describe a new product and the client looks excited, it's a great time to say, "Would you like ..." When you see they are totally not interested, you move to another subject. You need to be in charge of the situation without being overly dominant and to learn when to push a little more or when to back off.

Not only do you need to be good with words, but you must also present yourself well visually. If you're a representative of the beauty profession, "clean, neat, and attractive" are pluses. Charisma, or positive energy, draws people to you.

Working with some customers, you'll find timing is crucial. You sometimes find customers who are unhappy and ready for a change with your products and distributors. That timing can also be due to attending a workshop or show where they were presented with new products and opportunities.

"Sales" is the sharing of enthusiasm. Be consistent and ask frequently. You may hit at the right time when they are ready for a change.

The slower business months are a great time to help customers dust products, move them forward, set up educational programs, and make suggestions for new display ideas. Explain to them, "Now is a perfect time for education. Let me set up in-salon training sessions!"

A good sales consultant can help grow a customer's business through promotional and marketing ideas. They are dedicated to the salon's success. Let's face it, if the salon grows, so does their sales as well as yours. Sales consultants share incentive programs with salons. Often these incentives are created by goals and quotas set forth by the manufacturer and the distributor. If you want that salon to increase volume with you, show them how by putting it down on paper. The biggest way to increase a salon's income is retailing! The information in Book 3 of *Salon Success Secrets,* about retailing, is extensively covered. It doesn't matter what services a tech performs, retail sales can be included.

Another way to grow business is to help the salon increase their hair coloring business. If the salon is weak in this area, recommend upcoming color workshops or in-salon education. Create a plan of action for the salon with the owner's help. Either of you can present it to the staff. Merchandising and marketing people can assist you too.

When someone is ready for some big changes, remodeling, going into a new line of products, or opening a new salon, make an appointment with them. It can be at the salon or out to lunch to avoid interruptions. Bring brochures, prices and information with you. Have some ideas to present when you meet. Start-up promotions will give them the largest value for their dollar. Let them know all their benefits. If you know what they may like to purchase, have literature to hand them. Visual aids, pictures and samples will increase your sales. It's easy for people to say "no," so ask, "Is there any reason you would *not* want ...?" Listen to your customers' needs.

Your biggest obstacle when selling to salons is financial. They usually have as many bills as income. Some will make the decision then and there if the funds are available and some will want to think about it. Either way, follow up. Give some more benefits and don't be afraid to ask for the order. Customers expect it. If they did order and you know they will receive a large start-up order Wednesday morning, for example, call them that afternoon to make sure they received everything they needed. If you learn something is on back order, call them to let them know. They may choose to wait or substitute. If they don't hear from you, they may substitute with one of your competitors. Before you walk out of the salon, ask, "Is there anything else I can do for you today?" The "Oh, yeah" answers would have been missed opportunities.

Sometimes you'll have the chance to detail (travel to salons) with manufacturers' representatives or educators. Their experience with the products they market can greatly aid you in getting products into salons. If the salons are already carrying their products, the representatives can help the clients with product knowledge and how to increase sales.

Let customers know what you like or recommend. When you tell a customer you use a product you're showing them, you can see in their faces that you have established more credibility with it.

When you conduct yourself in a truly professional manner, salons will pay more attention to you. When you're trying to sell, if the salon people ask questions, act pleased (it indicates you're interested). Repeat their questions with something like, "Is this the only question you have that stands between you and ownership of these products?" If the customer has more than three issues, write them down, then answer all three. Continue with, "Is that a satisfactory answer to your questions?" Then to close the sale, "Is that fair enough?"

When asking questions, use positive words, such as "understand, proven, health, money, save, new, love, discover, truth, proud, profit, deserve, happy, trust, fun, security, advantage, faith, hope, easy, guarantee, right, results, comfort, value, vital, positive and benefits." Negative words to avoid are "deal, cost, pay, contract, sign, try, lose, worry, loss, hurt, death, mad, sell, sad, price, buy, decision, hard, difficult, liable, obligation, failure and pitch."

Beauty Supply Sales Clerk

If you're considering working in a beauty supply store, you have many of the same responsibilities as a distributor sales consultant, except the customers come to you. It is important to be informed on products. Customers expect you to know something about everything.

Some beauty supply clerks may give professional advice that creates bigger problems for customers. Someone called me in pain because the store clerk recommended artificial nail primer to get rid of fungus because the clerk heard it had an extra fungus-fighting agent in it. The acidic primer set her finger on fire and gave her a chemical burn. Luckily, she called me to find out how to neutralize the primer so it would not continue burning her. This was a professional item that should not have been sold to her since she was not a licensed nail tech. No advice is better than bad advice.

Some beauty supply stores sell to the public, and some only sell to the professional techs. The job typically consists of assisting customers, cashing out sales, stocking supplies, dealing with paperwork, making deposits, setting up educational events, making deliveries and cataloguing inventory.

If you decide to work in a beauty store, it is recommended that you read the manufacturers' support literature. It is also beneficial to attend educational seminars in-house and out. This is especially good if the store is on quotas to increase sales. It's an enjoyable way to work with salon professionals. Especially if you are a student wanting to meet the right people and have regular access to education.

~Section 2~

Selecting a Great Salon to work in!

9

Can This Be
Your Dream Career?

Once you've selected a profession and a school, what's next? Enroll and begin! The best way to get started in school is to associate yourself with other motivated students who share your interests and goals. Those who are eager to learn and attend class regularly are the ones who typically move forward in the industry.

I always volunteered to participate in special events for every opportunity to try out or see new things, not to mention making new friends and professional connections. I volunteered to do hair and makeup for beauty pageants, high school plays, fashion shows, local theater, TV shows, and community events that entailed dressing up, such as medieval fairs and parades. Not only were they a blast, but the recognition and new customers were a great bonus.

Use your spare time to research useful material. Professional magazines, styling books, cassettes and videos are excellent teaching tools for schools and salons. I suggest creating your own educational manual from items you collect. Put articles and flyers with product information from manufacturers into three-ring binders. When you find yourself feeling bored, go to the library. Ask your distributor sales consultant and store managers if they have things to give or lend you.

Part of excelling as a student involves taking notes, making drawings, taking pictures, making use of the school's library and reading everything you can get your hands on pertaining to your field. While writing this book, I pulled out all my notes I'd saved over the years from the training sessions I attended. It's amazing how much we can learn AND forget. I've used those notes over the years to aid me in my salon and school. Doing so has refreshed my memory, too, about implementing things that were not workable then, but are now.

Do the most productive thing you can at every moment. I like to surround myself with people who want to succeed. When I was in school, there was a group who hid in the back to avoid working. I don't think any of them got very far working in a salon. Stay in the thick of things so as not to miss an opportunity to learn what the instructor explains to a student working on a client. Be eager to do clients.

Students, Forge Ahead!

What's next? Uh-oh, working on clients. ... YIKES! The best way to excel as a student is to be eager to learn! Never be afraid to try something new. Remember, amateurs built the *Ark* and professionals built the *Titanic*. When clients go to beauty schools for services, they UNDERSTAND you are learning. Once in a great while, I'll have a client who picks apart every detail of a student's work. I let the client know that they are welcome to go to a regular salon and pay full-price if they would prefer a more professional service. Most of them return anyway, so they must be satisfied. Many salon owners advise, "Do not wear your feelings on your sleeve, because some people will hurt them." Enjoy the rest of the clients who are fun to work with, because there are so many of those!

When working with clients, sometimes some techs can be too rough or too gentle with massages on the body, scalp, feet, face or hands. Washing hair, brushing hair, and doing facials require a firm, relaxing pressure that feels good. Many students are afraid of hurting people, so they perform some procedures too lightly. The client may think

51

the student lacks confidence. I made an "I'm Afraid Nickel Jar." Every time I hear a student say, "I'm afraid," I point to the jar (I should actually make them PUT a nickel in it). As often as I hear it, it could create a good retirement fund for me! ☺ A tech with confidence is not wishy-washy when touching someone. This comes with just a little practice.

The same goes for filing on nails. Most students are so afraid of hurting people, that they file too lightly and use a half-inch of the seven-inch file. This creates more irritation on the cuticles, causing discomfort. I explain to them that a brand new file used near a cuticle is what causes most cuts. If you're unsure, just ask your client, "How is my touch?"

Some people are excited about school, but need a job in order to pay for it. I suggest they try getting a job in a salon or at a beauty supply store while in school. It gives them a head start in the beauty business, exposes them to learning from other professionals and allows them an opportunity to see how they like working in a salon as a future tech.

Note: When paying school tuition, remember to pay with checks. This becomes your proof of payment. With so many students and so much paperwork, losing data can occasionally occur. If someone else is paying for your tuition, make sure that YOUR name is written boldly on the check. There have been times when people left a check on my desk at my school and I didn't know whose account to credit.

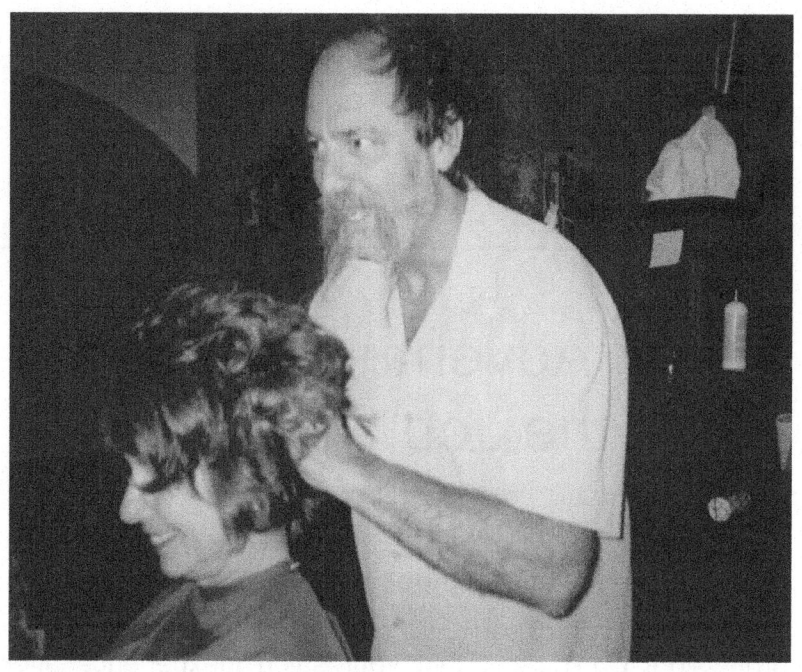

Cosmo Easterly, Ocala, FL.

Started in the salon industry in 1976. His accomplishments:
manufactured a hair cutting tool called "The Sculpting Knife", wrote a
permanent wave book titled "Permanent Setting", research and
development with hair color, and his hair and skin care product lines
called Cosmo, Mizar Series.

He has a true dedication for helping stylist grow in their salon career!

10

Adventures of the Job Search

Fresh Out of School ... Where Do I Go?

Selecting a great salon will set the foundation in your new profession! Don't fret about your salon inexperience after graduation. In some cases, salons prefer a fresh tech right out of school so that they can train and mold them. Look for progressive salons with growth. If the decor looks twenty years outdated, that's a clue that the salon's education may be, as well. Part of the 75% failure rate in the beauty profession is caused by a graduate's first job. If the experience is unpleasant, then failure is likely since they want out.

Amanda had fantastic talent and a slightly shy but very sweet personality. She went on one interview and accepted a job at a new salon. She hated her first salon experience. Her boss intimidated and embarrassed this fragile new graduate. Less than a year later, Amanda was looking for someone to buy her nail supplies because she no longer wanted to be in the profession. After a bad experience, too many graduates will leave the profession they have just entered. Don't give up! Move on to a more comfortable workplace.

Selecting the best salon for you needs a little homework. I suggest students make a list to help with the selection. Here are some key points you may want to consider before accepting a position:

1. Ask about the salon's reputation. Talking to distributor sales reps, local beauty supply stores, past employees as well as customers, can enlighten you. You'll get mixed comments, so go with the majority viewpoint. Your instructors may be able to guide you, if they are familiar with the job market in your area.

2. What products or techniques does the salon use? If you have preferences, ask what types the salon uses. If they insist you use a product you don't like, there will be a conflict.

3. Ask how long the salon has been in business. I don't recommend a brand-new, non-established salon for your first choice, especially if you're new in the profession and without clients. At least 90% of new salons close before they ever reach their second year. You could find yourself locked out with all your possessions inside if they owe money. An exception would be if the owner has extensive experience in salon management, they have a full clientele, enough staff members working there having a full clientele, or there are no or very few salons in t he community.

4. If you're trying to decide on where to work, particularly in your own small town versus traveling to a larger town where there the population is larger, work in your own community. You'll come in contact with people to build a clientele from. Invite people you know and meet to come and try you out. You're more accessible to clients if they only need to travel 10 minutes versus 45 minutes. There is also less competition in very small towns. You'll be a big fish in your own small pond instead of a small fish in a large pond.

5. Is the owner a great tech as well as a good leader? A tech wanting to become a salon owner can be the best at her trade, but running a salon is a different proposition. It's important for a business owner to have the natural ability to be: a technician (for example, a hairdresser), an entrepreneur (a dreamer), AND a manager all in one. A brand new salon always sounds fun and exciting, but longevity, with at least three techs with more business than they can handle, speaks for itself.
6. How many technicians are present and are there enough overflows to make a new tech necessary? Some salons have too many non-busy techs. This will make building a clientele difficult.
7. Does the salon sell retail products? If you want more money in your pocket, selling retail is the way to go. Do they have training programs to help you with product knowledge and to increase retail sales?
8. Is the location in a high-traffic area? If the salon is out of the way, has low foot traffic coming in, or is hard to get to, it is more difficult to build a clientele.
9. What kind of turnover of clients, as well as techs, do they have? If people stay there for years, it shows stability.
10. What type of clientele do they have? If you have a preference for teens, retirees, baby boomers, men, women, or a tattoo and piercing parlor, make sure you're going to be comfortable with the people you'll be working on. Family salons have it all—men, women, and kids. The atmosphere of people and music you enjoy can make you happy and upbeat. Don't select a place you'll dread walking into each day.
11. Does the staff "play" well together? You don't want to work at a hostile salon. I can tell what kind of manager and staff members are in a salon by the atmosphere. The behavior of the salon owner will dictate what will be acceptable for everyone else. If an owner gossips, swears, smokes, drinks while working or argues with people, the rest of the staff and clients will follow suit. This also includes

appropriate dress in the salon. The owner acts as a team leader. It's a good idea to pick a salon that has someone you can respect. Salon owners can also be ineffective managers, unorganized, emotional, or moody.

12. How does the staff behave as you walk in? Look for pleasant faces when you enter.

13. What kind of social action dominates the salon? If you like to work in a more private situation, as in a day spa, you will not be as happy in a salon where all the work stations are together and people interact and socialize. When you get a group that's in an all-open area, that's what commonly happens. Some salons have divided work areas for more one-on-one interaction between the tech and the client. Some salons have a pace that is speedy and energetic, others are calm and relaxed. If in doubt, ask.

14. How busy is the salon? You can even go into a salon as a client. I would do this on a Friday morning, because that's usually the busiest time. If there is hardly any business for the existing staff, this is a bad sign. If you had difficulty getting an appointment, then you have an idea about their need for a tech.

15. Are you offering a service that no one else is doing? For example, if you're a massage therapist, esthetician, or nail artist going into a hair salon, check and see if there is a demand for these services. There should be enough existing clients to help you build your clientele. Example: Four busy hairdressers should be able to supply a new nail artist with clients.

I learned the hard way what it feels like to experience most of these unfavorable circumstances—at the first place I worked. I'm not sure if you can call it work since I never did actually earn any money. I became friends with a lady at school whose boyfriend was opening a salon. They asked me to go to work for them and I was excited. But there were a few glitches in the plan that I didn't know would become obstacles for me.

The boyfriend left Daytona to open the salon in New Smyrna Beach where he lived. He had no management training or experience. Since the new salon was 40 minutes away from his established clients, almost none of his clients followed. My friend was fresh out of school, with no clients. They opened a brand-new salon in a location that had a lot of beach driving traffic, but almost no foot traffic for walk-ins. They didn't have enough money to purchase most of the necessary supplies for work. They weren't able to do much advertising on their tight budget.

Since the three of us had not lived in town very long, we didn't know many people. They were planning to do the hair. He cut my hair one day and it was the worst haircut I'd ever had, even after he fixed it. I became less and less impressed with his abilities as a business owner. I was supposed to do the nails to start out and as they grew, add services like hair and skin care. I did one client and waited to find out when I should come in again. They needed all the money they could get, so ended up doing the nail clients and expected me to wait until they were ready for me, four months later. In the meantime I did some research and took a great job with another salon I worked at for years until I moved away.

Seven years and much continuing education later, I moved to Ocala with a bit more knowledge under my belt. I knew what I was looking for. I first looked through the phonebook to see the ads of various salons. This tells you something about the way they advertise for new business. I went to a local beauty supply store and talked to the staff to get an idea of the salons' reputations and listened to what people said. One phrase someone offered as a criticism actually appealed to me: "They are snobby there." This means they are a very high-end salon and charge more for services. I decided to put it on my list of salons to check out. I personally preferred a salon that serves more financially favored clients than budget clients.

A high-end salon charges more and pampers a specific class of people. Their clients expect better treatment. Other salons offer the same services at a fraction of the cost. Some salons focus on volume. These salons charge less and get more people in and out each day. You have to decide which salon best fits your personality. Other salons focus on retailing and have requirements on the amount you must sell each month. If you feel uncomfortable with selling, you either catch on quickly or feel stressed out worrying about quotas. Some techs enjoy the high-paced, busy salons while some prefer a calmer, two-chair salon.

I find that people who are the hardest working are also the hardest playing. Techs like me thrive on working in a busy salon on one person after another. In between clients, I'm reorganizing the storage area, telephoning about marketing, and work on keeping the place efficient. A busy, hectic salon may overwhelm people who are more passive; they may prefer a slower place to service each client.

All salons have a large variety of clients. It's up to your specifications as to what type of atmosphere you prefer to work in. There will always be clients who prefer quality and others geared toward price, some who like a busy, active salon, and some who want peace and quiet.

Did I get sidetracked again? OK, when I went job hunting, I picked a slower salon day like a Tuesday or Wednesday so they would have more time to give me a moment to chat. I dressed up, had my hair, nails, and accessories looking dramatic for my first impression. When I walked into the salon with my résumé in hand, I noted the atmosphere. I said I was not in a rush when the salon owner/manager showed some interest in talking to me. This allowed me time to check out the salon.

When their phone rang and they scheduled appointments, I peeked at their appointment book as they flipped pages, to see if the staff was fairly busy. If I saw lots of staff members with lots of openings for the present week, I knew there was not enough business to go around.

I walked around, checked out the retail sales material, talked to the staff and customers, and let them know I was looking for a job. If most of the staff seemed receptive, this made it more inviting. People love to share their viewpoints. When customers talk up the salon, this makes it even more inviting. Some owners/managers took the time to talk to me. If they were busy and I was interested, I asked them if I could set up a time to talk with them. Once I had the interview and understood all the compensation and benefit plans, I was better equipped to actually select the right job.

Most salons are privately owned and don't have the same benefits as chain salons. If you have dreams of a real career, don't reject one job offer that promises you an excessively high commission or salary over one that presents less percentage. A salon offering a higher commission often has less customers for you to build from. It may be a bribe to take a job that offers nothing more than a chair. You'll be on your own, with no future. Listen for a key phrase like "We'll train you."

If you want to find out if a potential employer would be amenable to helping you learn more in your new profession, check with your school's director or owner about inviting that potential employer to come in as a guest instructor. You'll know right away if they have the patience to help you grow.

Choosing the type of clients you want to work with will help you find the right salon too. If you want a high-end clientele, a walk-in salon that offers discounted prices will not satisfy you. If you want to specialize in men's haircuts, then find a salon/barbershop that has many men who come in.

New in my career, I worked for Mary at a second salon. She had a full-service salon that I was interested in. Her salon would expose me to a variety of services to help develop my techniques and expertise. Mary did nails, hair, waxing, skin care, body treatments, makeup, electrolysis, and many other specialized treatments. She had all the equipment and supplies needed for me to work with. I soaked in as much as I could hold, learning from her.

I knew starting out would be slow. But the more services I could offer, the more business I would gain. I also had the opportunity to gain management experience. Mary was out of town part of the week doing these specialties, so I was left to run her salon. I worked with five other staff members who taught me their specialties. I gained much new knowledge there.

Scott Brown owner of Scissorhands, Ocala, FL

My hairdresser, Scott Brown of Scissorhands in Ocala, Florida, shared some valuable thoughts with me. "You need to always keep an open mind to the spectrum of possibilities to explore, and a willingness to try everything. People often have these preconceived ideas of their future in this profession. Ideas learned can later become a passion. On the other hand, fear may hold you back from trying different avenues. Some have a mental image of greatness. Some graduate disappointed."

Compensation (Rent or Commission)

"Should I go on rent or commission?" "How will I get paid?" "I found a job, the rent is only $70 per month. Is that good?" You may encounter owners/managers who discuss booth rents or commissions. I recommend you don't start on rental without a clientele. It's better to start out on commission because the owner will invest in getting you built up much more than someone wanting techs to help pay the rent. If an employer makes half of what you make (this is typical), they are interested in helping you build, since it will also increase their income.

Some techs think 50% is a lot. But when it comes to paying the overhead, it is totally fair. Most owners will be happy to explain where the other part of "your" percentage goes. Owners are responsible for a monthly building payment, electric, phone, advertising, water, insurance, licenses, cleaning, bookkeeping, office supplies, bathroom supplies, repairs and maintenance. You may even find owners who are willing to pay you 70%, but there may not be enough business to build from.

Don't be surprised if a salon offers you a contract, especially if you rent. Some contracts will prevent you from working in the future within a certain distance from where you'll be working for them, for a specified amount of time after you'd leave them. Make sure you have someone knowledgeable about beauty salon contracts explain your options. If you can live with most of the points, you may be able to negotiate the ones that make you uncomfortable.

If a rental situation comes with an established clientele, there is no guarantee they will stay with you. If the ultimate goal for you and the salon is to pay rent, I recommend starting out by paying the salon 50% of what you make each day or week until that 50% is more than your rent for at least two months. For example, if your rent will be $100 a week, make sure your income is over $200 each week. Then you can be assured you're making enough to cover your rent without losing money. This arrangement makes it fair for all involved until you have built up your clientele. Note: If you work for yourself or are an independent contractor, you should be covered by liability insurance.

A select few larger salons as well as chains may have the ability to offer advancement to your career with competitive salaries, ongoing paid educational programs, medical insurance, sick days, vacation days, holidays, incentive bonuses, and employee recognition programs.

Some progressive, medium-sized to large salons may have staff members willing to teach you. Search out all your options, ask other techs in the area, and read the series of *Salon Success Secrets* books to help guide you through the job searching and success process.

11

Success in Time!

Working with Teri in New Smyrna Beach was a blast. She was old enough to be well experienced, yet young enough to make working with her enjoyable. What a talented individual she was, I thought, as I watched her in awe. She was unbelievably creative with hair and had many trophies to prove her abilities. Her confidence was astounding without being arrogant. She had an excellent rapport with her clients. They all loved coming to see her. She entertained them with her stories and vibrant sense of humor. Sometimes her clients had to wait 45 minutes. But they permitted it because her talent was irreplaceable.

She hired great talent and we learned from each other. We worked together as a team. We had many established salon clients who came to many of the staff members for a variety of services. Everyone looked forward to walking in that salon each day.

I worked for some of the best employers and some of the worst and learned many valuable things from both. Even some bad employers can teach you something so valuable that it will remain as an important lesson your entire career. One I worked for did a good job on advertising to bring new business in. They can also teach you what NOT to do by their example. This same boss would have to continually do a lot of advertising because he treated people like they didn't matter. He was rude, would not say hello or acknowledge them, and say unprofessional things. The clients would not return. If someone in the salon said something to him about it, he would tell him/her where he/she could go. OUCH! I decided not to follow his example!

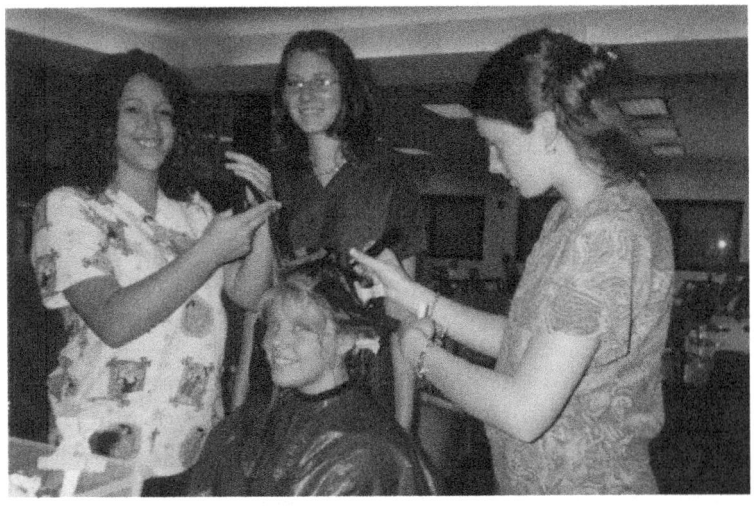

Somer Roth, (left to right), Stephanie Klinger, and Tara Neumann, Central Florida Community College Cosmetology students, practice perming on fellow student Kristy Donaghy, (sitting in the chair).

Enrollment in cosmetology schools is at about half of what it was two decades ago, creating a shortage of licensed techs. Yes, salons need more licensed people to fill their chairs. When salons are looking for employees, they will often contact schools. Remember that salons look for those who "play well" with staff as well as students and clients. Your dependability and attendance are reflected in what you say and do. Having a warm personality makes all the difference in success. The best salons strive to find graduates who are helpful with clients and who willingly take on extra tasks.

It's terrific to see people who take pride in their work and who want to work with others. Over the years I've seen people in the profession with little talent, but who still make a good living. What they lack in dexterity, they make up with communication and sales. I have also seen new graduates who create better work than most long-term professionals. So everyone has an opportunity to be successful in the salon.

Like most other competitive professions, you may encounter cutthroat or devious people. Do not let them discourage you. Most professionals and salons aren't like that. Professionalism, passion, and foresight in the beauty industry come from the heart. According to the Cosmetology Boards, 75% of students don't make it through school or through their first year in the profession. I feel there are too many students who get discouraged too soon because they don't know enough yet. They have not experienced that point of confidence that takes time to develop. (Can it be true? Someone disliking one of the most enjoyable professions to be in?)

Students should exchange phone numbers in order to call each other when one of them stops attending school. They can keep each other revved up. A little determination and a good education will increase your odds. I wrote this series of books to help you with both.

Chain Salons

Chain or franchise salons can be a wonderful way to get more education right after you graduate or if you're getting back into the beauty field after being out of it for a while. Chain salons often offer training programs, salary, and commission as well as benefits and incentives. A salon chain has at least five related salons. Go to www. naccas.org, then "chain salons" to find stores like J. C. Penney, Burdines, Fantastic Sam's, The Hair Cuttery, Toni & Guy, Regis, Supercuts, and Trade Secret to research the possibility of working for one of these chain salons.

Chains certainly have an advantage of setting up shop in prime real estate locations. Mall developers are more likely to seek out national chain salons rather than local salon owners for large shopping centers. They like the chain's track record; it is financially stable and its brand-name appeals to shoppers. You can learn the art of retailing (which is required more by chains) and get some advanced skills and techniques under your belt.

12

Dress for Success

LOOK PROFESSIONAL! Do you feel that appearance plays a part in getting a job in this profession? Absolutely! A person will dress 33% better for an interview than daily on the job. People have walked into my salon wearing a dirty T-shirt, cutoff shorts and a pair of old flip-flops asking for a job. This frightened me! I tell people, "If you wear it to the beach, at the gym, or to work around your house, don't wear it here at the salon." Ponder what impressions you have of people around you by their appearance.

One of my clients shared something she heard during a makeup class: "There are no ugly women, just lazy women." As I thought about the women I observed in my salon and around town, it was apparent which people took great pride in their appearance.

How can people improve their appearance? The first problem I hear from people getting started in this profession is, "I don't have enough money to go shopping." But when they do go shopping, they seem to buy more of what they already own, such as shorts, T-shirts or other less professional casual clothes. You can find business casual clothes for the same prices on sales racks. You can find excellent bargains at consignment shops. Dress for the position you want to be in.

Remember that the salon will attract what it represents, including you. Outrageous people are usually found working in outrageous salons offering services such as body piercing. Remember that you will be spending lots of time at your new workplace and you want it to match who you are.

Most people have nice outfits hiding in their closets. Break them out. If you wait too long to wear them, they'll be out of style. When Lynn started working for me, she dressed very casually. I tried to convey to her that it was affecting her business. At times when I was unavailable, I would suggest to my clients that they go to Lynn for their service and explained how wonderful her work was. In response they would say, "Well, you'd never tell it by looking at her." It hurt her to hear that, but until she saw how important appearance was, she would never see how it affected her income. If you *choose* to be in the beauty industry, remember that your own appearance does play a big role. Just look at the makeup counters in mall department stores.

Wearing a closed, long smock can be a solution if you want to stick with your T-shirt and shorts (popular in Florida). A person doesn't have to be dressed in formal attire to be well groomed. One can appear well groomed in jeans and a T-shirt if this fits the occasion. A nice belt and shoes, along with your hair, nails, and makeup looking sharp, are beautiful accessories.

A big part of your appearance is affected by your mental attitude. Being tired or stressed out shows in your face and posture. Healthy eating and drinking influence your skin and complexion. When I'm having a good day, I'm often complimented on something I'm wearing. When I'm having a rough day, it shows and, I assure you, no compliments are offered.

My best friend Patty in high school usually had hairstyles that drove me insane because she was always "growing it out." I would ask, "To what?" She would shrug her shoulders, with no response. I would say, "You can at least trim it and keep it looking nice in the process." Sometimes people see our appearance differently than we see it. If someone does compliment you, "Thank you" is the best response, not "Oh, I can't stand my ..."

Make sure your hygiene is up to par. Not taking a daily shower or not using a deodorant and being in direct contact with people can be offensive. When you talk face-to-face with people, your customers may critique your hair, teeth, nails, and feet. If you use perfumes, do so in moderation; a third of the population is sensitive to it. Wear jewelry tastefully. If it takes a whole cigar box to store what you wear each day, you're probably overdoing it.

Makeup must always be suitable to the time and place. No makeup for women is unacceptable, if you're serious about being in the beauty business. People can always improve their appearance, their personality, their skills and talents ... if they want to!

13

Rev Up Your Résumé

Remember that there are many salons looking for techs. Don't be too concerned about writing a résumé. Almost all the people going into a salon looking for a job don't even present one. But if you want to be better than the rest of the applicants, here's how to develop one.

A résumé should be brief and to the point. It should not be too plain or too fluffy. Phrases such as "a challenging position," "contribute to your organization/goals," and "advancing growth" make a difference. If you want to be noticed, be unique. State your specialties. Rather than listing the typical job descriptions and responsibilities, let the potential employer know how you have made a difference for your past employers. It shows that you're ready to do more than just put in hours. State community projects, languages you speak, and certifications and awards you've received.

It is recommended that résumés be no longer than one page. Avoid repeating the same information. The interview will allow you to supply more details. Your hobbies and interests are only important if they are relevant to the job.

Think of a résumé as a commercial for a great movie. It should entice the viewer to want to contact you for an interview to see the rest. The entire résumé should include highlights that grab the reader's attention. Use minimal words by avoiding "I," "me," "the" and "an" when writing the facts. Viewers with many applications quickly glance through them and look for key words that fit the job they are trying to fill. A few well-chosen words are more valuable than lots of fluff.

The résumé starts with your basic information: name, address, phone number and e-mail address. More personal information is not needed in most situations. When mailing your résumé out of town (especially for jobs that relate to public speaking), you can include a professional photo.

The first heading is the objective that states your best skills relevant to the job you're applying for. These may change depending on what the company is looking for. Yes, you may need to alter your résumé from job to job. If you have not developed special skills yet, leave this out.

The next section, the background, should give quick, concise details of your experience. You don't have to use complete sentences. You can use verb phrases, such as "Organized student training for competition"; "Created demo material for instructors" and "Led client-building competition."

Your employment (or experience, if lacking an employment history) should start with your most current job and work backward. Your experiences can include educational events you attended related to the profession. If there are valid gaps in the dates, such as attending school or having children, that situation can be listed with the dates among the other job dates.

Next will be your education.

Finish with the summary. This will emphasize your skills, how advanced they are, and how they relate to the position you're applying for. If you know what the employer is looking for, this can give you an idea of what to state.

You can add references or state they are available upon request. You can also state your future intentions. Do you plan to work part-time or full-time? Will you also be attending school while working or taking extra time off to be with family? I have hired people, thinking they would be working full-time while they planned on working 15 hours a week. This created a conflict for both of us. I had to start the job search process all over again because we didn't meet each other's needs.

When you have jotted down all your notes and organized them, you can type your résumé yourself or have a friend or a professional service help you. If you create it yourself, have two others proofread it to check for clarity and mistakes. See sample résumé in Appendix C.

If you write a cover letter, it should be adjusted to each job as well as the business you are applying to. It should also reflect your résumé. See sample cover letter in Appendix D.

Approach the Salons of Your Choice

Once you have chosen the type of salons you want to work in, it's time to make contact. Stop in and meet the salon owner or manager. Find out if they are hiring. Even if they were not looking, sometimes they will make room for someone who impresses them. Ask to set up a time for an interview. If you would like to practice for an interview, find someone to role-play with. If you're nervous, you can ask a business professional, an instructor, or a human resource person to help you with correct interview replies and behavior.

When you get the application, fill it out entirely. If you do have a résumé, attach it. In filling out your application, you can write "See Résumé" on the application in the areas asking for duplicate info. Include past jobs and references. Graduates with no salon experience are concerned about filling out an application. The owners/managers know you're a new tech. Keep in mind that they're looking for people with a favorable work ethic; for example, punctuality, cleanliness, professionalism, honesty and working well with others. The beauty profession is primarily based on interactions with others, more than talents. You can be the best tech in the world, but if your rapport with others is brash, you will lose business for the salon. The salon owner or manager will review your application accordingly.

If an appointment is set up for an interview, BE PUNCTUAL. An interviewer will most likely check your references and job history. Be honest, always; getting caught lying is the worst. While you're at an interview, be courteous and show enthusiasm for the job! Have a professional attitude as well as a sense of humor ... and SMILE. Be prepared to do demos of your work. You may want to offer to do a demo on the interviewer especially if you are doing nails, facials or massage. Let them know you're ready to work as soon as they want you.

After the interview, follow up, follow up, and follow up. Some people get jobs just by being a pest. This is the truth! Lynn came to me three times for a job. I was not interested in her because of her appearance. But she kept coming back, so I knew she really wanted to work with me. She was like a sponge; she wanted to learn everything I could throw at her. She ended up being a great asset for many years, until she moved across the country with her new husband in the military.

While I'm on the subject, if you're on a military base, your license from any state is good while working on the base.

A Fail-Safe Interview

Since most salon owners (or managers) don't interview people on a regular basis like a human resource director of a large company does, most will not go for the big questions. The majority will go by first impressions and intuition. They are concerned about your personality since that is almost more important than technical skills. They look for people with an enthusiasm for learning and working.

They want to know if you'll show up each day with a willingness to work, and do it full-time! They want someone who will be part of a team rather than someone who just looks out for number one or someone they'd have to force out of a chair to service a client.

To get to know you, an interviewer prefers you answer questions with some detail. So there will be less yes-or-no questions and more fill-in-the-blanks. These open-ended questions could be real salon scenarios to see if you have common sense answers or if you fall apart under pressure.

These are some questions they may ask, along with responses they look for:

1. What are a few of your best strengths? They are looking for an answer that will help the company. So answering "Long-distance runner" should not be your first choice. But, "While I'm attending athletic events, I enjoy marketing myself as a massage therapist" would be appealing. It shows you market yourself.

2. What are your two biggest weaknesses? Yes, you are allowed—and expected—to have some. Answering "None" shows you may be afraid to be honest.

3. What obstacles have you faced at previous jobs? The interviewer wants to see if you admit to problems, and if you have problem-solving skills.

4. How would you describe your last three bosses and working environments? If you talk badly about all of them, it's a reflection of you—not getting along with others.

5. What would your last two bosses (or instructors) say about you? Would they want you back? If you're wishy-washy or indirect, it shows there were some difficulties.

6. Why did you leave your last three jobs? They understand situations like moving away, having a baby, moving up or into a new (salon) career. But if you blame each of the companies for your issues, it's a reflection of your inability to adapt or get along. So, personal reasons as the answer for each will be a cause for concern to the interviewer.

7. Have you ever been fired from a job? A few phone calls can verify the answer, but they want the truth from you. They are looking to see if you understand and accept why you may have been fired. The interviewer wants to know if you learned from the experience.

8. Do you typically get along with almost all, some, or very few of your co-workers and why? This business involves much contact with others and they want to make sure you're a "people person."

9. What kind of schedule would you like to work? If you want to work less than 20 hours a week or 10 a.m.-2 p.m. each day, you won't be a great asset to the salon. "I can be here whenever you need me" is the most favorable response (if it applies to you).
10. How many days have you been late or missed work in the past two years? Dependability is the concern here.
11. Explain why you're suited for this job. They are looking to see if you can think on your feet.
12. What motivates you? Some people are strictly motivated by money. Interviewers are looking for multiple answers versus one focus.

If any of the questions they ask are tough, take a deep breath, relax (but don't slouch), collect your thoughts and do the best you can. If someone is interviewing for the president's position for IBM, he will feel the pressure too! It's not always the answers they are interested in, but to see if you can handle pressure with good communication skills. If you have ever seen a courtroom scene on TV with the person on the stand losing their cool by spurting off, then you understand what they're trying to avoid. They want someone with self-control. When someone is under pressure, they show their real emotions.

Once the interview is over, you can ask questions too. You may want to discuss compensation. Do they pay commission or have booth rental? You can also use the 15 questions listed under "Selecting the Best Salon for You" covered in chapter 10. This can be a guide as to what is important to you. If they ask you to return to demonstrate your talents, smile ☺—you passed the most difficult part!

14

Wow, I Found a Fabulous Job!

Your first day of work at a new, unfamiliar salon in a totally new profession can be tough. But we all have to start somewhere. Start out on a good note. Introduce yourself to your new co-workers. Heck, bring in a pan of brownies! They want to know who the new person is, and offering a treat is a great icebreaker. They're wondering ... *Is she/he any good and will we like her/him?*

Feel out your co-workers and find out who is willing to let you watch or even go as far as teaching you. If they let you watch and ask questions with one client, don't assume you can do this with all clients. Subtly ask them if this is a good time to watch, and look at their expressions. Some clients are more private and would not appreciate an audience. If they know you're excited to learn, they may call you when they are doing a technique you'd enjoy learning.

You also want to make a good impression on clients, so don't forget to introduce yourself to them, especially if they are on display for you. Offer them a drink, if available. The time may come when their regular tech is unavailable. If they thought you were a "nice person," they will give you a try.

You need to learn the fine line between being eager to learn and being a pest. Watching body language is a very good indication. If someone is trying to turn their face, eyes and/or body away from you, that is an indication they would like to end the conversation or be left alone. Others who smile at you and ask you questions are inviting you into their presence. Additional knowledge of body language can give you added perception with clients and will be worth the time you spend reading about it.

It is imperative that you, now a new professional, understand that your time at the shop is crucial for success. Once you are in a salon, you need to stay focused. A key point many salon owners regularly state is that people starting in this profession need to understand they aren't going to make $500 a week fresh out of school. This is an accomplishment resulting from hard work, continued education, and developing talent.

Even if your appointment book is not full, being present at the place of business will bring you clients. You need to be at the salon as much as possible to gain all the new clients you can. Some techs want to be called only if a client wants to book a service, or want to spend only 15 hours a week working, which is not realistic for building a full book. You need to be available for the new client when she or he is eager for the new service! The average salon professional makes close to $25,000 their first year working full-time. Using the techniques I describe in the *Salon Success Secrets* series should make you way above average!!

Setting Up Your Work Area

The other part of starting a new job is making sure you have the proper supplies. You can use the list from chapters 2-8 as a guide. Price lists from the manufacturers whose lines you'll carry can also give you an idea of necessary items.

Beauty World , Ocala, FL

When you are beginning—and in most students' and beginners' situations, you will not have a lot of money—pick and choose what's most important. Save your pennies. As you start to make money, do your research and find out what will work best. As you purchase the most important tools you'll use every day, seek quality. It can make a difference in the end result of your work.

Order items like good shears and brushes. Things like double-density bristled brushes made of first-cut quality boars' hair that actually polishes the client's hair while you use it.

A Kolinski red sable brush for artificial nails can move your work up to another level. Comfortable equipment for your clients to relax upon (without holes) is a plus. Quality is a representation of the work you do!

Next will be general supplies you may need in a salon.

Basic Items:

Work station (and chair)	Pens & pencils
Client records	Ticket book
Business cards	Record keeping setup
Price list	Outlets
Brochures	Proper lighting
Appointment book	

15

Focus on Your Goals

Now that the basic information about the salon industry has been covered, I'd like to finish up by creating your new beginning. The first step in deciding on any new career is setting goals. The secret of getting ahead is getting started. So let's start with something simple. Write down some short-term, easy goals. I'll wait while you get a pen and paper.

Goals are made when you put them in writing, not merely by wishing for something. Thoughts, positive or negative, grow stronger when fertilized with constant repetition. Some people spend their time "talking" about what they want to do.

Now ...

Where were you 5 years ago?

Have you moved ahead?

Will you still be there in 5 years?

A student, Ellen, 31, would come to school steadily for a few weeks, slow down, stop for a couple months, and repeat this pattern. Her friends and family encouraged her to stick with it. Her personality and skills would make her a great tech. Her mom said she had always had trouble completing things, but hoped this would be different. When Ellen said she could not afford it, her mom even offered to pay for her schooling. She was the Queen of Excuses. Unfortunately, years later, Ellen is still unhappily working minimum wage go-nowhere jobs.

Goals have to be "ardently desired." You want it so bad, you grit your teeth stating "I really want this!" So, pin up your written goals someplace you can see and read them regularly. You should see my bathroom mirror!

Remember to set your own goals. If not, others will set them for you, like one of my students, Jennifer. Her dad decided she should get a job delivering mail. Since she enjoyed working with others, being alone in a car would not provide her with a happy career. So she made a goal of working in a salon. She went to the phonebook and called a few salons to inquire about schools. She called my school, amongst many, for information, then checked them out. Within a week she started at my nail school and loved it. She is even happier now that she is making money at a fantastic job.

Once you have set, worked at, and completed some goals, it's great to go back and see how many you've successfully achieved. You'll work on more challenging goals once you have more confidence. Then start working on long-term goals, like going to school or deciding where you would like to work. If you're looking for adventure, your goal might be to work on a cruise ship or out of the country. We all need to imagine our goals and visualize them for ourselves.

The opportunities to find a great job are numerous in the wide-open salon market. Take your time and select YOUR best opportunity!

The only way to create success in your life is to stay focused. Think about what you want and visualize it! See it! Feel it! Believe in it! Make your mental blueprint and build on it. Have faith that you can succeed, and anything is possible!

To receive salon newsletters, go to www.kimstevens.net

I would like to invite you to read more of the **Salon Success Secrets** books to guide you through innovative yet practical ways to increase your volume of customers and make your job better. Develop expert communication skills that will make you irresistible. Utilize the steps in this series of books and watch how quickly financial rewards follow.

Book 2 will cover: client building, client retention, makeovers, catering to clients, salon environment, client consultation, client forms, salon specialties, professional image, communication, customer service do's and don'ts, phone etiquette, and clients' special occasions.

Books 2 and 3 in the series cover most of what you'll need to know to prosper while working in salons. Utilize the steps in this series of books and watch how quickly financial rewards follow.

Book 3 will show you ways to gain innovative, real salon ideas and techniques guaranteed to sharpen your performance and increase your income. Whether you're a new salon professional or a veteran, these practical solutions will power up your creativity and enthusiasm. Enjoy what you do (a whole lot) more. Book 3 will cover: increasing your income, marketing yourself, solving a problem with a product, financial freedom, the power of knowledge, beauty expos, setting up a book camp, creating a salon association, salon pricing, the psychology of selling, staff communication, maintaining your health, merchandising, and extensive retailing techniques.

Books 4, 5, and 6 will cover going into business for yourself. It addresses rental, salon and school ownership from start to finish. These books should start evolving in 2005.

Appendix A

Cosmetology Boards

Cosmetology Board Directory -
http://www.naccas.org/StateBoard/index.htm

Note: Call "information" (the area code of the capital city) plus 555-1212 and ask whichever board you want to be licensed under if you don't find what you need in the appendix. Some professions, such as body piercing, will fall under the health department.

Alabama Board of Cosmetology
cosmetology@aboc.state.al.us
http://www.aboc.state.al.us
100 N. Union St., Suite 320
Montgomery, AL 36130
(334) 242-1926

Alaska Division of Occupational
Licensing, Board of Barbers &
Hairdressers
license@dced.state.ak.us
http://dced.state.ak.us/occ/pbah.htm
P.O. Box 110806
Juneau, AK 99811
(907) 465-2547

Arizona State Board of
Cosmetology
1721 E. Broadway Rd.
Tempe, AZ 85282-1611
(602) 784-4539

Arkansas State Board of
Cosmetology
darlene.burrow@mail.state.ar.us
101 E. Capital Ave., Suite #108
Little Rock, AR 72201
(501) 682-2168

California Bureau of Barbering &
Cosmetology -
http://www.dca.ca.gov/barber
400 R Street, Suite #4080
P.O. Box 944226
Sacramento, CA 95814
(916) 445-7061

Colorado Board of Barbers &
Cosmetologists
barber-cosmetology@dora.
state.co.us
http://www.dora.state.co.us/barb
ers_cosmetologists
1560 Broadway, Suite #1340
Denver, CO 80202
(303) 894-7772

Connecticut Dept. of Public
Health
410 Capitol Ave.
Mail Stop #12 Application Dept.
P.O. Box 340308
Hartford, CT 06134
(860) 509-7569

Delaware Board of Cosmetology
& Barbering
http://www.state.de.us/research/
profreg/cosmotol.htm
861 Silverlake Blvd. Canon
Building, Suite #203
Dover, DE 19904
(302) 739-4522

District Of Columbia Dept. of
Consumer & Regulatory Affairs,
Board of Barbering &
Cosmetology
614 H St. N.W., Room 904
Washington, D.C. 20001
(202) 727-7474

Florida Dept. of Business &
Professional Regulation
http://www.doh.state.fl.us/mqa
1940 N. Monroe St.
Tallahassee, FL 32399
(850) 487-1395

Georgia State Board of
Cosmetology
237 Coliseum Dr.
Atlanta, GA 31217
(912) 207-1430

Hawaii Dept. of Commerce &
Consumer Affairs
Board of Cosmetology
1010 Richards St.
P.O. Box 3469
Honolulu, HI 96801
(808) 586-2708

Idaho State Board of
Cosmetology
csimpson@ibol.state.id.us
http://www2.state.id.us/ibol/cos.htm
1109 Main St., #220
Boise, ID
(208) 334-3233

Illinois Dept. of Professional
Regulation
http://www.dpr.state.il.us
320 W. Washington St.
3rd Floor
Springfield, IL 62786
(217) 782-0458

Indiana Professional Licensing
Agency State Board of
Cosmetology Examiners
http://www.ai.org/pla/index.htm
302 W. Washington St.
Rm. EO-34
Indianapolis, IN 46204
(317) 232-2980

Iowa Dept. of Public Health
Professional Licensing Agency
321 E. 12th St., 5th Floor
Lukes Spades Office Bld.
Des Moines, IA 50319-0075
(515) 281-4416

Kansas State Board of
Cosmetology
714 S.W. Jackson, Ste 100.
Topeka, KS 66603
(785) 296-3155

Kentucky State Board of
Hairdressers & Cosmetologists
dena.moore@mail.state.ky.us
111 Saint James Court, Suite A
Frankfort, KY 40601
(502) 564-4262

Louisiana State Board of
Cosmetology
lsbc@state.la.us
11622 Sunbelt Court
Baton Rouge, LA 70809
(225) 756-3404

Maine State Board of Barbering
& Cosmetology
anne.l.head@state.me.us
www.maineprofessionalreg.org
State House Sta. 35
Augusta, ME 04333
(207) 624-8603

Maryland Board of
Cosmetologists
mbrown@dllr.state.md.us
http://www.dllr.state.md.us
500 N. Calvert St., 3rd Floor
Baltimore, MD 21202
(410) 333-6320

Massachusetts Board of
Cosmetologists
zane.b.skerry@state.ma.us
http://www.state.ma.us/reg/boar
ds/br/default.htm
100 Cambridge St., Rm. 1406
Boston, MA 02202
(617) 727-9940

Michigan Dept. of Consumer &
Industry Services
Attn.: Cosmetology
P.O. Box 30018
Lansing, MI 48909
(517) 241-9201

Minnesota Dept. of Commerce
Licensing Division
Attn.: Cosmetology
licensing@state.mn.us
http://www.commerce.state.mn.us
133 E. Seventh St.
St. Paul, MN 55101
(800) 657-3978

Mississippi State Board of
Cosmetology
P.O. Box 55689
Jackson, MS 39296-5689
(601) 987-6837

Missouri State Board of
Cosmetology
P.O. Box 1062
Jefferson City, MO 65102
(573) 751-1052

Montana Dept. of Commerce
Board of Cosmetologists
compoleos@state.mt.us
www.com.state.mt.us/license/pd/ind
ex
111 N. Jackson
P.O. Box 200513
Helena, MT 59620
(406) 444-4288

Nebraska Dept. of Health &
Human Services Regulation &
Licensure Credentialing Division
hhsinfo@www.hhs.state.ne.us
http://www.hhs.state.ne.us/lis/lis.asp
P.O. Box 94986
Lincoln, NE 68509-4986
(402) 471-2117

Nevada State Board of
Cosmetology
nvcosmbd@govmail.state.nv.us
1785 E. Sahara Ave., #255
Las Vegas, NV 89104
(702) 486-6542

New Hampshire State Board of
Barbering, Cosmetology and
Esthetics
http://www.state.nh.us/cosmet
2 Industrial Park Dr.
Concord, NH 03301
(603) 271-3608

New Jersey Board of
Cosmetology & Hairstyling
http://www.state.nj.us
P.O. Box 45003
Newark, NJ 07101
(973) 504-6400

New Mexico Board of Barbers &
Cosmetologists
P.O. Box 25101
Santa Fe, NM 87504
(505) 476-7110

New York Dept. of State
Division of Licensing Services
licensing@dos.state.ny.us
http://www.dos.state.ny.us
84 Holland Ave.
Albany, NY 12208
(518) 474-4429

North Carolina Board of
Cosmetology
ncs0963@interpath.com
1201 Front St., Suite #110
Raleigh, NC 27609
(919) 733-4127

North Dakota Board of
Cosmetology
cosmo@gcentral.com
1102 S. Washington St.
Suite #200
Bismarck, ND 58504
(701) 224-9800

Ohio State Board of
Cosmetology
http://www.webtest.state.oh.us/c
os/index.htm
101 Southland Mall
Columbus, OH 43207
(614) 466-3834

Oklahoma State Board of
Cosmetology
http://www.state.ok.us/~cosmo
2200 Classen Blvd., Ste #1530
Oklahoma City, OK 73106
(405) 521-2441

Oregon Cosmetology
hdlp.mail@state.or.us
www.hdlp.hr.state.or.us/bhhome
.htm
700 Summer St. N.E., Ste #320
Salem, OR 97301-1287
(503) 378-8667

Pennsylvania Cosmetology
Board
cosmtol@pados.dos.state.pa.us
124 Pine St., P.O. Box 2649
Harrisburg, PA 17105-2649
(717) 783-7130

Rhode Island Dept. of Health
russells@doh.state.ri.us
http://www.health.state.ri.us
Division of Hairdressing &
Barbering, Rm. 104
3 Capitol Hill Rm. #104
Providence, RI 02908
(401) 222-2231

South Carolina Board of
Cosmetology
http://www.llr.state.sc.us
P.O. Box 11329
Columbia, SC 29211
(803) 896-4494

South Dakota Cosmetology
Commission
sdcosmo@sd.cybernex.net
http://www.state.sd.us/dcr/cosm
o.html (top)
500 E. Capitol
Pierre, SD 57501
(605) 773-6193

Tennessee State Board of
Cosmetology or State Board of
Barber Examiners
http://www.state.tn.us/commerc
e/cosmo/index.htm
500 James Robertson Pkwy.
Nashville, TN 37243-1147
(615) 741-2515

Texas Cosmetology
Commission
catherine.nahay@txcc.state.tx.us
http://www.txcc.state.tx.us
5717 Balconies Dr.
P.O. Box 26700
Austin, TX 78755
(512) 454-4674

Utah Division of Occupational &
Professional Licensing
http://www.commerce.state.ut.us
160 East, 300 South
Heber Wells Bld. 4th Floor
P.O. Box 45805
Salt Lake City, UT 84114-6741
(801) 530-6628

Vermont Office of Professional
Regulation
patkins@sec.state.vt.us
http://www.vtprofessionals.org
26 Terrace Street
Montpelier, VT 05609-1106
(802) 828-2373

Virginia Dept. of Professional
Occupation & Regulation, Board
of Cosmetology
cosmo@dpor.state.va.us
http://www.state.va.us/dpor
3600 W. Broad St.
Richmond, VA 23230-4917
(804) 367-8509

Washington Dept. of Licensing
& Professional Licensing
Services Cosmetology Section
plssunit@dol.wa.gov
http://www.wa.gov/dol
405 Blacklake Blvd.
P.O. Box 9026
Olympia, WA 98507-9026
(360) 753-3834

West Virginia Board of Barbers
& Cosmetologists
1716 Pennsylvania Ave., Ste #7
Charleston, WV 25302
(304) 558-2924

Wisconsin Dept. of Regulations
& Licensing, Barbering &
Cosmetology Examining Board
wisc-web@badger.state.wi.us
http://www.state.wi.us
P.O. Box 8935
Madison, WI 53708
(608) 266-5511

Wyoming Board of Cosmetology
jvialp@missc.state.wy.us
2515 Warren Ave., Ste. 302
Cheyenne, WY 82002
(307) 777-3534

Appendix B

Massage Boards

http://www.thebodyworker.com/massagelawsandregulations.htm

Alabama Board of Massage
Therapy
660 Adams Ave., Suite 301
Montgomery, AL 36104
(334) 269-9990
Fax: (334) 263-6115

Alaska Dept of Commerce &
Development
P.O. Box 110606
Juneau, AK 99811
(907) 465-4855

Arizona License Service
251 W. Washington 3rd Floor
Phoenix, AZ 85003
(602) 364-0720

Arkansas State Board of
Massage Therapy
103 Airways
Hot Springs, AR 71903-0739
(501) 623-0444
(501) 682-9170

California Dept. of Consumer
Affairs
400 R State St. Suite 1040
Sacramento, CA 95814
(916) 445-1254

Colorado Dept. of Regulatory
Agencies
1560 Broadway Suite 1550
Denver, CO 80202
(303) 894-7855

Connecticut Dept of Health
150 Washington St.
Hartford, CT 06106
(860) 509-7603/7566 or
(800) 842-0038

Delaware Office of the
Governor
Cannon Building, Suite 203
861 Silver Lake Blvd.
Dover, DE 19904
(302) 739-4522 ext. 205
(302) 744-4500

District of Columbia, Massage
Training Inst.
John A. Wilson Building
1350 Pennsylvania Avenue NW
Washington, DC 20004
(202) 727-1000
(202) 244-2280

Florida Dept. of Health
4052 Bald Cypress Way
Bin #C01
Tallahassee, FL 32399-3251
(850) 488-0595/6021

Georgia Examining Board
166 Pryor St. SW
Atlanta, GA 30303
(478) 207-1430

Hawaii DCCA-PVL
ATT: Massage
P.O. Box 3469
Honolulu, HI 96801
(808) 586-2699/3000

Indiana City Controller/Finance
Dept.
2221 City County Building
Indianapolis, IN 46204
(317) 233-0800

Idaho Occupational Licensing
Board
2404 Bank Drive Room 312
Boise, ID 83705

Illinois Dept. of Professional
Regulation
http://www.dpr.state.il.us
320 W. Washington St.
3rd Floor
Springfield, IL 62786
(217) 782-0458

Iowa Department of Public
Health, Bureau of Professional
Licensure
Lucas State Office Building
5th Floor
Des Moines, IA 50319-0075
(515) 281-4422

Kansas
No license required

Kentucky
No license required in 2003
The state is in the process of
forming the massage board

Louisiana Board of Massage
Therapy
PO Box 1279
Zachary, LA 70791
(225) 658-8941
Fax (225) 658-8946

Maine Department of
Professional and Financial
Regulation
#35 State House Station
Augusta, ME 04333-0035
(207) 624-8624/8603

Maryland Dept of Health
4201 Patterson Ave.
Baltimore, MD 21215-2299
(410) 764-4738

Massachusetts
No license required
Contact your city or county
health department
Or (617) 635-5326

Michigan
No license required
(517) 241-9288

Minnesota
No license required
Contact your city or county

Mississippi
No license required

Missouri State Board of
Therapeutic Massage
3605 Missouri Boulevard
P.O. Box 1335
Jefferson City, MO 65102-1335
(573) 522-6277
Fax: (573) 751-0735

Montana
No license required
Contact your city or county
(406) 444-3665

Nebraska Credentialing
Division, Massage Therapy
P.O. Box 94986
Lincoln, NE 68509-4986
(402) 471-2117

Nevada
Contact your city or county
For specific licensing
Requirements

New Hampshire Department of
Health and Human Services
129 Pleasant Street
Concord, NH 03301-6527
(603) 271-4592/5127
Fax: (603) 271-5590

New Jersey Board of Nursing
P.O. Box 45010
Newark, NJ 07101
Fax: (973) 648-3481

New Mexico Massage Therapy
Board
2055 Pacheco Street, Suite 400
Santa Fe, NM 87504
(505) 827-7013
(505) 476-7090/7089

New York State Board for
Massage Therapy
State Education Building
2nd Floor East
89 Washington Avenue
Albany, NY 12234-1000
(518) 474-3817/3866

North Carolina Board of
Massage & Body Works
Post Office Box 2539
Raleigh, NC 27602
(919) 546-0050
Fax: (919) 833-1059

North Dakota
State Board of Massage
Bismarck, ND 58504
(701) 258-3359
(701) 872-4895

State of Ohio Medical Board
77 South High Street
17th Floor
Columbus, OH 43215-6127
(614) 466-3934
Fax: (614) 728-5946

Oklahoma
No license required
Contact your city or county

Oregon Board of Massage
Therapists
3218 Pringle Rd. SE, Suite 250
Salem, OR 97302
(503) 731-4064 or 365-8657

Pennsylvania
State Board of Cosmetology
P.O. Box 2649
Harrisburg, PA 17105-2649
www.dos.state.sa.uf
(717) 787-8503
(717) 783-7142

Rhode Island Division of Health
Services Regulation, Health
Professions
3 Capitol Hill, Room 104
Providence, RI 02908
(401) 222-2827
Fax: (401) 222-1272

South Carolina
Massage/Bodywork Therapy
PO Box 11329
Columbia, SC 29211-1329
(803) 896-4588
Fax: (803) 896-4484

South Dakota
No license required
Contact your city or county

Tennessee
425 5th Ave. North
Nashville, TN 37247-1010
(888) 310-4650
(615) 367-6393

Texas Department of Health,
Massage Therapy Registration
Program
1100 West 49th Street
Austin, TX 78756-3183
(800) 942-5540
Utah Dept of Commerce
160 E. 300 South
Salt Lake City, UT
(866) 275-3675
(801) 530-6628

Vermont
No Regulations
Virginia Board of Nursing
6606 West Broad St., 4th Fl.
Richmond, VA 23230-1717
(804) 662-9909

Washington State Department
of Health Professions
1300 SE Quince Street
P.O. Box 47860
Olympia, WA 98504-7860
(360) 586-6351

West Virginia Massage Therapy
Licensure Board
200 Davis Street Suite 1
Princeton, WV 24740
(800) 871-7265/(304) 487-1400
Fax: (304) 487-1460

Virginia National Certification
Board for Therapeutic Massage
and Bodywork (NCBTMB)
1735 North Lynn Street
Arlington, VA 22200
(800) 296-0664
(703) 610-9015
Fax: (703) 610-9005

Wisconsin Bureau of Health
Professions - Massage Therapy
PO Box 8935
Madison, WI 53708-8935
(608) 266-0145

Wyoming
No license required
Contact your city or county
health department

Appendix C

Résumé

Heidi Brown
123 Mars Road
Hollywood, CA 94705
(309) 555-4444 (home)

Objective: Position as a nail artist in a growing salon.

Summary of Qualifications:

- 2 years' experience in a grocery store as clerk, checker, and cashier.
- Excellent reputation with customers as a competent, knowledgeable and helpful professional.
- Honest, reliable, and productive.

Customer Service:

- Developed a reputation for excellent customer service by:
  a) acknowledging the customer's presence;
  b) greeting customers in a friendly manner, and giving them full attention;
  c) taking time to answer a question or find someone who could.

Employment History:

2000 – Present: Retail Clerk, large supermarket, Hollywood, California

Education:

Cosmetology School, 2002, Great Looks Community School
Hollywood High, 2000, graduated in the top 10% of my high school class

Appendix D

Cover Letter for Résumé

January 19, 2005

Dear Ms. Bolder,

Enclosed is my résumé outlining my desire to enter the salon industry as an entry level Salon Assistant. The majority of my experience has been that of interacting with the public and in customer service. My talents were highlighted during high school as an art major and I was active in many clubs. As the president of the Art Club, our group received city recognition for beautifying our community in 2003.

I have lived in Hollywood, California, for fifteen years and have interacted with the community, including volunteering at the hospital. My hard work, ethics and discipline to get the job done have been acknowledged by my former employers. I look forward to hearing from you in the near future.

Sincerely,

Heidi Brown
123 Mars Road
Hollywood, CA 94705
(309) 555-4444

If you enjoy *Salon Success Secrets* by Kim Stevens, there's more!

You can be added to a mailing or e-mail list to be informed of future books, tapes and speaking engagements. If you would like printed material, details regarding a salon consultant/evaluator, staff and education development, motivational speaker, help in starting a salon or school, advice about equipment, design, or financing, or if you would like to share your ideas, please contact Kim.

Go to **www.kimstevens.net** or complete the postcard below, cut it out, stamp and mail.

- - - - - c u t - - a n d - - m a i l - - - - -

Name_____

Address_____

City_____ State_____ Zip_____

Email_____

Phone_____ Phone_____

Areas of interest:
{ } Seminars   { } Books & Audios   { } Printed material
{ } Consultant { } Other_____

- - - - - cut - - and - - mail - - - - -

Kim Stevens
1959 Big Crane Loop
Port Orange, FL 32128

Made in the USA
Monee, IL
07 July 2026

56551274R00059